Under The Precious Umbrella

Under The Precious Umbrella

SELF PORTRAIT JUGGLING SAMSARA AND NIRVANA

Roberto Valenza

nine muses books
seattle/pensacola 2001

I desire to thank the westerners who helped me when I entered into the Tibetan Vajrayana family. Keith Redman, Monk Karma Lesche, Robert Beer, Hetty MacLeise, Keith Dowman, Noel Cobb, Tabla Paul, all translators, the Nuns of Kopen.

The poets and seers: Ira Cohen, Angus MacLeise, Petra Vogt, John Chick, Terry Turnoff, and especially my companion through all the travel years, Tancha (Valenza) Whitfield (Knight).

My sincere thank you now in the 21st century goes out to the translators of the Tibetan Buddhist Dharma whose work has advanced in quallity along with the growth of Vajrayana Buddhism in the west. My sangha thanks go to Erik Pema Kunsang (Erik Hein Schmidt) for translating the brilliant books from Rangjung Yeshe Publications.

The last and biggest thank yous: to margareta waterman who put out the three chapbooks which have now grown into the entire collection. She is the one who has brought this book to life. To Donna Lee who uncovered my demons, and taught me yoga, true generosity and a sharing of grownup love. And to my mom, Agnes, and my daughter Tia.

Roberto Valenza

THIS BOOK IS A GIFT OF THE ELF FUND

isbn 1-878888-39-0

nine muses books
3541 kent creek road
winston, oregon 97496
mw9muses@teleport.com
robertovalenza@hotmail.com

GARUDA WITH HAT PHOTO BY IRA COHEN

INTRODUCTION

Roberto Valenza, Akashic agent & charter member of the Kathmandu Starstreams Gang, is a poet who specializes in the real deal. No armchair Buddhist, he has devoted himself to working through the Dharma first hand, body & soul. A poet of the crazy wisdom school, a solo streetman, he is also an accomplished singer, an Italian crooner who has mastered traditional styles of Indian and Tibetan chanting & Thanka painting. His Rock & Roll Hell's Kitchen rhetoric underlies his deep understanding of the spiritual path & makes these poems ring like Quasimodo's bells in the long night's dreaming. This is the payoff, the result of a life spent in pursuit of raw truth through devotion. These poems are poems of prayer, flares of illumination clothed in robes of gold. Tap dancing on the funeral pyres of earthly longing, his knowledge is founded on his willingness to give himself completely to the rag people, the teachings of his rat guru, to the most real & unreal. This is the art of non-discrimination carried to the highest power as in the practice of Padmasambhava. What is it if not the song of the self when there is nothing left to say? He shows us Buddha in everything. "I shut my eyes. I shut my words. May I treat everyone I meet like fragile butterflies." It is not too late for the star to love us. See the monkeys fall like stones, have compassion for the moth sold to the devil's jar, go with a flashlight into the darkest depths. If you try, it will be yours; the rainbow, the Shiva moon. The poet cries out,"Oh shroud me in your golden invisible." Incurable and all healing, these are poems of the Way—animated by life itself...Poets are not like other people. Singing the Skull Mantra, Roberto Valenza relentlessly polishes the diamond of love in these poems. This is his sadhana. This book should be eaten *al dente*. May the clouds grant us the asylum we crave. Roberto, I salute you.

OM AH HUNG

Ira Cohen
June 27, 2000

POETRY REVIEW 2001

Much in the Indo-Tibetan style of spontateous realization poetry or Doha songs, Roberto Valenza cuts through the a+b=c clutter of traditional Western thinking to arrive at insight (*prajna*) by a naked awareness of flux and the moment. Presented through his own everyday enlightening experiences and woven with a highly original use of language, ***Under the Precious Umbrella*** is the collision of different worlds and realms, sentient beings and religious practices, and the resulting exchange or transformation of energy. Here the reader not only meets with spiritual awakening, guru yoga, visualization, mantra, the accumulation of merit, dedication and rejoicing—but also Shiva/Kali's dance of dissolution and the Buddhist underlying belief of impermanence and emptiness.Like the “crazy wisdom” teaching of Drukpa Kunley, some of Roberto Valenza's skillful means as seen in the poems *Blood Coverage* and *Monkey Falls* are directly juxtaposed to the ‘fragile butterflies’ of *Cave of Guru Padma* and the compassionate *Wings and Wound.*

E Ma Ho! These poems have an extremely powerful, evocative and other-worldly array of images that portray Roberto's journey or quest past the knowable borders of our own time and space.

Lee Harris
Tibetan Buddhist Monk
Seattle

publisher's note

Roberto Valenza is among those whose life was changed by the good fortune of encountering buddhism. an american, born to the streets, to a beautiful tenor voice and a lot of undirected talent, to rock and roll, to the corruption and materialism of the times. for seven years he lived on swayambhu hill in katmandu, learning the ways of thangka painting and mantra singing and the buddha-mind, attending ceremonies and initiations and spending much time in the personal company of high lamas.

and returned a dedicated artist, a musician, painter and poet who carries the vajra-dharma thunderbolt back into the same real-life american world he came out of...

Under the Precious Umbrella, first released in a series of chapbooks out of seattle in the nineties, is the record of his katmandu life, his immediate responses to what he saw and experienced, the inspiration of the himalayan buddhist reality.

this work bridges the gap between intellectual knowledge of buddhism and the direct down-home application of it to one's own imperfect self.

margareta waterman
nine muses books

DEDICATION

REFUGE

In the Buddha, the Dharma, and the supreme assembly
I take refuge until enlightenment.
By the merit of generosity and so forth
May I attain buddhahood for the welfare of all beings.

Namo, in the lord guru, the sovereign of all buddha families.
In the yidam deiity, the source of accomplishment,
And in the dakinis, who dispel all obstacles,
I take refuge in the Three Roots.

Namo. In the empty space, Dharmakaya.
In the cognizant nature, Sambhogakaya,
And in the manifold capacity, Nirmanakaya,
I take refuge until enlightenment.

DEVOTION TO ONE'S OWN LAMA-GURU

In all my lifetimes may I not be separated from my lama.
May I use to the full the high teachings he gives me.
May I reach the Bodhisattva levels and attain the good qualities of the path
Soon may I attain the realization of the Buddha who holds the Vajra

OM MANI PADME HUM
OM AH HUNG VAJRA GURU PEMA HUNG

---

taken from *Rangjang Yeshe Chant Book*, received from Chokyi Nyima Rinpoche retreat, Rangjang Yeshe Gomde, Leggett, CA, 9/2000

MORNING PUJA

A rumble against the forces of
negativity.
Humble soldiers of Buddha, singing
the bells of wisdom.
Sweet smoke burns over Samsara City.
Prayers are made for the suffering of all
things alive.
A general beats the drum, and gives no
commands.
Compassion banners with the holy
Guru Shakyamuni smiling,
float above our heads

SALUTATIONS TO THE SUPREME SILENCE

Om-Namo salutations from the hawk to the crow,
        the crow won't stay long
    the hawk thinks he'll allow him a pause.
Om-Namo salutations from the sea to the land,
    wave's hands curl, knees of water kneel,
and a grace-filled prostration lays itself on the shore.
Om-Namo   with a gentle roar,
        sending a creative impulse
      positive   negative
          over the earth,
            namo,   namo,   namo,
              namo,   namo,   namo,
Om-Namo
salutations from the body mind song to the open air
        to the breezy wind blowing past
Om-Namo   caw, caw, caw,
        or a heated dove's coo,
        crow song, cat song, ant song,
        man song, om-namo salutations
        to funny concept-chew-will-I-zations

namo namo namo namo
  Om Muni Muni Maha Muni Soha

KALI CHAKRA INITIATION

(given in Bodh Gaya by the Dalai Lama)

I

The mandala is full of flesh and the heat of some
burning circle in something called the sky
in a time called afternoon.
Also the circle, the time, the heat, the mandala, the is,
and the something are all names which in their
true nature are void.
Sitting peaceful without much wisdom, hands in prayer,
requesting peacefully as possible, “may I enter?”
This is fantastic, just sitting here at the tip of a golden
dorje and looking in at the palace could be enough.
I’ll just sit here and wait for the answer.
No more can be said about this inner initiation
into the mandala of the Kali Chakra.

II

If I had the knowledge of the true existence and non-existence
of pain
I could sit here waiting, picking at my foot until all
the skin peeled off and then pick at the flesh
until the bone showed . . . . .
and after I picked everything into little specks
of bloody flesh and bone I’d still be sitting
here waiting for permission to enter.

III

When you got, you don’t care too much about getting, but you
care about protecting.
When you don’t have, all you can feel is wanting.
Surely the only thing to go through these is renouncing.
To renounce correctly one should know these
objects in their true nature,
then in pure motive love it all.

IV

If I'm allowed inside, why don't I just always live there,
moving out the walls with every step and
learning to become my newly won form,
letting its righteousness seep into the ordinary one
and transform it into the incredible
resurrection of the clear one,
dualistic union
blissful voidness
with no end.

V

To reinforce yourself or others' dumb tricks is to be an
ignorant fool.
Also to become angry at yourself or others' dumb tricks is
also to be an ignorant fool.
One doesn't have to think that the way to be polite is
through reacting.
Om In the basic truth about relative things one thing leads
to another.

VI

Noticing a light in the door, and names on the steps.
If I could use the little energy which is used
for physical comfort for enlightenment
I'd be through the door
prostrating to the throne and the
holy body, speech and mind of the lotus born.

VII

An answer falls out of the air,
"It is using your mind that will
get you to the other shore."
USE
TO STAY AWARE AND USE IT MORE,
VISUALIZE A BLISSFUL WORLD
IN WHICH YOU ARE
A POSITIVE PURE BEING
ADD TO THE VISUALIZATION GOOD
UNSELFISH DEEDS
AND BECOME THE ABSOLUTE VISUALIZATION
OF PURE HELP.

VIII

The Dalai Lama places a living smile on the
coming alive visualization of Avalokitesvara,
Chenrezi.
His wisdom is clear and simple like a Buddha's.
I'm sure he would say, "I am a poor teacher."
But his words and physical manifestations
show us different.
Plus he is the Kali Chakra.

CHENREZI

CHILD MAN KARMAPA AT PRAYER

under the waterfall below where
Guru Rinpoché left a hand print in stone

What with all the wrath
and fang teeth
sharp nails holding blood
filled skull cups
what with all the magic
pointed eyes
and
glory filled robes

What with all of this
who would believe that
when you pray alone
you pray like
a little boy
hands together
your face filled
with moist emotion.

Ah Karmapa Khyenno

YOUNG MAN KARMAPA
TRADITIONAL TIBETAN PHOTO

AWAKE POEM

every morning I awake with the birds
          or a crazy frog who lives next door
I awake and remember I'm dying
and I can't see a reason or an example
of anything stranger

every morning I feel so solid
          so here and making progress
and then I remember it's all for nothing
          because if you're alive you're dying
so what in this life can be so important

here I am again
looking at my hands,
"may my hands be blessed by not hurting
anything"

the birds stop singing for a moment
          and give the crickets a last chance
                    to speak to themselves
                              and say goodnight
as we all say good morning.

TIBETAN FOREST

under the great mountain Lang Tang
in the Himalayas

This autumn forest
with many colors of fallen leaves
and ferns is the forest where
Tibetans go to return with wood
to warm their homes.
I can hear them sing a high tone song
as they return from wood cutting
after leaving the communal kitchen.

On coming down from the high peaks
just to step into their village one is blessed.
Their sweetness is something never felt before by me.
I love these people.
They are kind without needing kindness in return.
I feel accepted like I've returned home
after being at war for a hundred years.

The power and the energy one gets from noticing the
ghostly white mountains that float above this
dream village,
"each breath is *amrit*, sweet as an angel's kiss,
my mercury feet of wings, each breath is *amrit*,
sweet as a loved one's lips."

Homage to those who are trying to help.
A fire glows in a little cave high in snow cold land.
The fire they send in prayer is cherished unknowingly
in the hearts of everywhere.

TIBETAN FOREST

TO THE POINT

our moment is a shadow
archetypes in a maze world
all these eyes staring
wondering where & how to begin
the search

like magnets they are
attached
to anything resembling
a good mother
a good father
a good hitler

Hour Before Dawn
Cold and Wet Puppies
Mindless
Running Crying Around the Stupas

In the morning I throw
them some bread
A Monkey gets It.

LEARNING RAGA SINGING

I love my singing teacher (guru)
He tells me without art
Man is a beast.
So we sing
and if someone blows us up
the pieces
will sing.

NEPALESE MOUNTAIN POEM (the rag people)

the rag people come
and shed twenty pounds of cloth
their dust & dirt bodies show scars
of years of inbreeding and work
they are the cloth mole people
the wood smoke smell people
smiling through their smallpox scars
they are the rock house livers
the walk up and down people
the thanksgiving for every parasite that crawls
each rag person carries their possessions
on a back of open sores
hello to the hard life smile people
born to live forever on the hard rock ground
goodbye to the rice potato people
with their dung smell houses
the rag people come
they shed a thousand pounds of dirty cloth
and sit in the sun taking turns
picking bugs from their hair
they laugh at me as I pass
feeling my mental head
the rag people would never do this
to themselves

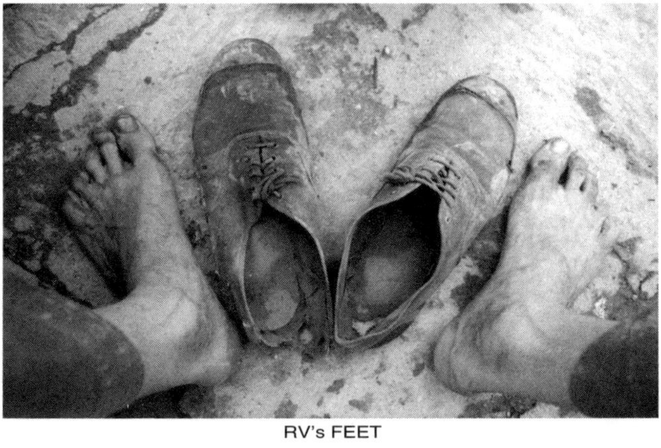

RV's FEET

WE PRODUCE OUR NEEDS

it is not too late here
to see one Saivite yogini
in the middle of the square
pounding her trident to the ground
speaking the sound OM
from a face somewhere beyond your vision
it is not too late to witness bloody sacrificial
masses in the light of day
even to be splashed by some of the juices
and leaving marks that stay for your lifetime
And then there's the death

a thing that is always being
carried down to the river
with just a thin cloth to hide
the features of useless flesh.

VOWS JINGLE

Precepts & Refuge
No killing, no stealing, no lying.
No Sexual Misconduct,
No Intoxicants.
How's a fella gonna
find any fun anymore

I shut my eyes.
I shut my words.
May I treat everyone I meet like they are fragile
butterflies.

NAMGYAL

(with Goenka at Vulture Peak)

Sitting, sitting, cross-legged, not moving
with-holding the primal scream,
going quietly beserk inside.
Pain is impermanent . . . one hour of sitting cross-legged
is endless til it's over,
then more again and start another hour,
slowly burning up the ignorance of deluded views,
clearing the stains from the pure unkown.
It's physician heal thyself,
probe deeper, deeper, disintegrate.
Rather hard to sit here for a span of time,
not moving, watching the sensations caused by
delusions, arise and fall.

Ha ha I laugh with tears falling on the inside,
aware that I'm suffering,
faking to the outsiders who are faking to me,
we all agree that
it's too much, too personal to show each other the
pain we are all feeling being separated from any
particle of lasting wisdom,
any true happiness.

Cave of OM AH HUNG VAJRA GURU PADMA SIDDHI HUM
(before leaving America i knew I'd find a cave in the Himalayas)

In the bushes where the rabbit shit is
    my direction to take a pee leads without direction
        straight to a cave
            where little prayer flags dance in the
            air.
At a sound I stop
    and look into the black mouth and hear the little birds
    talk of my coming.
Next flash is to sit and meditate
    a divine experience in a series of divine experiences.
OM AH HUNG VAJRA GURU PADMA SIDDHI HUNG sings
from the rock the natural fire pit the smoke flowing
out towards the glazier across the river.

Whenever time and life ongoing breaks apart the space
created is a feeling of strangeness when you're only a
fella with a past not a dealer in the ancient craft
of meditation.
Transcending solids, grandfather, father, mother and son
mountains smile down in their new white dresses,
they are dancing a polka in slow motion.
The sun mixes with liquid stone, my legs are like
a Siva Saddhu's, white and flaky like ash, my hands
remind me of an elephant's knee, dry and tough.
My lips are like my lungs worn by many kisses.
The landscape is illuminous bright crystal which the rays
of the sun hit and splash color in the refraction, but
my flesh has still a quality more, held up against the
peaks it looks fragile I know each wrinkle.

The Trinity plus me turn pink, grandfather's
beard turns to elephant tusks.
The power and energy one gets from noticing the ghostly
mountains floating above fills my ears with this message,
"Homage to those who are trying to help,
a fire glows in a little cave high in snow cold land,
the little fire they send is cherished unknowingly in
the hearts of everywhere."

I shut my eyes.
I shut my words.
May I treat everyone i meet like fragile butterflies.

US

(in song if there be inner rhythm)

We are the trigger to the gun
We are the center of our own mandala
How can we allow anything to control us?
We are the flash of life speeding through Life
once with our face
We are a sleeping Buddha
How can others cause us Suffering?
We are the source of everything we perceive
happening around us
we are the savior, the destroyer, the seasons of
the year
How can something make us eat the apple of ignorance?
EXISTENCE   NON EXISTENCE   BEING   NON BEING
THERE ARE SO MANY THINGS TO DO IN THE WORLD,
just because we don't do something anymore doesn't
mean we wouldn't do it again sometime
one doesn't repeat bad actions when one is totally
purified
we are the mouse of existence
we are the cat awaiting at the hole
how many times will we fall to the same bait
we are the fish hooked and enjoying being
pulled out of the void.

THE SPELL OF THINGS

Dancing masks of Evening
Ancient Growls in the Modern Night
Aging Tibetan Trumpets Blow Above
Army bugles blow below
Rumors Weirdly twist about the end of the
Dharmic East
Who can turn away the Angel of Death
Who is the essence of change of this Earth

Wild Beasts fight amongst the stupas
Screech Owls dive at Black Cats
Directly down from the Divine Love Temple
Sinister Figures Stand Under Street Lamps
A Few newly born sneak about praying for peace
Hoping not to be noticed in a
strange period of time and space
This basic pit full of beings of self-destruction
where suffering is something one can
find easily, and sensitivity hurts

MAO's ROAD

In china all the Buddhas are boiled down.

In 1954 they built a road
to Lhasa to make sure
the artillery would get there in time for 59.
Now behind the hill there's a road
being made from here to Lhasa
in time to make Padmasambhava more of
a seer than he's been.

Am I looking at the last years
of Swayambhu?
Like candle wax will the prayer wheels dissolve
into copper drain pipes for the
roofs of Mao or some other old fart?

Meanwhile the Nepalese King sits fat in a 1930's
sofa, smiling about barter with anyone
who'll trade a box of cigars
for a hundred pounds of peasant sweat.

CAGED BUDDHA

IGNORANT SON OF A GUN

Hamburger, leg of lamb, veal cutlet
    with pie on the side.
Black leather jacket, alligater shoes,
what made me think these creatures never felt?
The fly under the fly swatter.
So clear I can see me and my best friend
    keeping score of sparrows killed
or smashing sunfish on the sidewalk
    on a Sunny Sunday afternoon.
Now I'm afraid,
        Extreme fear!
What's gonna happen to me? It appears
    I must forget my little worldly pleasures,
        but I feel connected.
Oh well, this religion is just like all the rest,
    heaven, hell, saviors, what a lot of
        baloney.

Baloney, pigs head smashed with a hammer,
swung by a fella who sells meat on the
                                        corner.

REPLAY

May I sometime become pure smoke and drift up
  to some pure land where teachings rain
    from Buddha, Jesus, Arhants and pure beings.
The past is full of images of me as a hero,
  good though struggling, but today oh,
    repentance through realization of viewing
      the life I've led, not much joy without the
        greedy rat, much dirty alleys sneaking as
          a thief, needles dripping roses of blood,
            prisons of silent torture, singing songs
              for sex and fame, jealous love, on and on
                very uninteresting pornographic album
                  or novel.
Well tonight the altar is yellow, in it sits the Tibetan
    Maha Siddhi whose words are pure gold and
        sweet as the Bodhicitta Mayahana Teachings.
We are taking precepts,
rules on life for this life and future lives,
and it seems I may slide up that
chimney
yet.

DURING GURU RINPOCHE WONG AT MY HOUSE

beginning at: preparation of altar
  the gold swirls of the holy water vase,
    peacock feather top blasting up in colors
      turquoise eyes of feathers
        staring back at Lama,
    prayers and mantra,
    tsampa in brown hands molded
    into offering, (TSOK)
    calling on many deities in preparing
    place, altar, offering bowls, us,

water, flowers, incense, food, light, sound,
    strong odor of ghee (butter)
        with red herb color
        for red blood on Maha Kala terma,
Gosainkunda, Lang Tang, white mountain peak
    outside of window, Dorje Chang
blue sky out of window,
white mountain reflection on Lama's glasses
    his mouth open, bottom of teeth showing
        mantra cleaning the room

Tsampa (barley flour) made into offering pyramids,
    shapes of Mt. Meru,
lingam, herbs making blood pyramids
        and persian king coffins,
Mombo   Mombo
beads click from moving mantra mala
        I go to refuge to

    the precious Lama
    the Yidam
    all victorious Buddhas
    the holy dharma teachings
    all the compassionate Bodhisattvas
    and all those with the wisdom eye

OUR ALTAR ON SARASWATI-MANJUSRI HILL

Swayambhu Stupa through the small window
   Dhyani Buddha Palace of 3 kayas
      samadhi eyes
   looking back into my strange consciousness
as we pray to Manjusri & Saraswati.

Giggle inside of good meditation clearing
      cleaning room of demons, cymbal
    and drum an OM AH HUNG
    twisting terma for demons thrown
         out the window
      giggle again in brain
there is no one else in this room
      thinking the things I am
full with the thoughts of a wholly different
      nature than this puja
cymbals bring it all into the mandala
while compassion bells ring

victorious banners waved in front of altar
      smoke of incense
      strong mantras and prayers
      monkeys pulling to get in
         no chance,
      victory bells inside, outside the
perfect curve of Himal snow peak
      inside the perfect cup of Tea,
making perfect bowl of rice and
tough Buffalo meat,
      potato, carrot,

and offer it up to whatever image one
         considers pure
      without discursive thought

(during puja break 2 young monks reading
      Indian made Buddha and Hanuman comic books)

2 days after my nov. 7 birthday
on Saraswati-Manjusri Hill,
Swayambhu, Nepal

SOMA DRINKING DREAM STATE

Through the mist
    this me sees the trees drip
not quite hidden in the distance some part
        of the Himalaya range shows
        its face
Dogs bark
Some Myna bird and crows squawk
then instant shock quiet takes
        everything and fills
the hill with electric hail stones
As the rain drops part from the branches
        they appear as great white balloons
            and fall delicious
        to the beaten path below

MUSIC PRACTICE

Sitting down ready to begin
      again another day
            of practice,
the hot eastern sun
pulling at my powers.

I always have the aspect
      of death as my partner,
its energy looks over
my shoulder
as i strum the tampoura.

Curiously even though the feeling
      of death is strong
            I continue
the work
the creation of something
            from this creation
                  of flesh.

KALI BABA PHOTO BY IRA COHEN

MAHA KALA PUJA

MAHA KALA PUJA PHOTO BY IRA COHEN

ॐ MAHA KALA, dispel the enemies of the DHARMA

I simply must share what I know of what is going on inside Tibet and our attempts to keep up the pressure from outside it. China's government systematically cheats, murders, steals, and rapes the people and environment of Tibet. Forced abortion and sterilization, job, education, housing discrimination, cultural genocide, more than 600 monasteries destroyed, hazardous waste dumping and more than 1.2 million dead or disappeared. Some of what is going on today in occupied Tibet. So even though this book is about the beauty and magic of Tibetan Buddhism I find it impossible not to speak of Tibet's other horrible reality.

As I was a part of demonstrations in Seattle so I took part in one of the more important secret ceremonies in Nepal, the pre-Tibetan New Year cleansing of ignorance Maha Kala Puja. Two years in a row Hetty and Angus MacLeise, Tancha Valenza Knight, and myself were voted in by the monks to participate in this seven day retreat. What you will be reading all really happened, at least from where I was sitting.

Puja is a ceremony much like going to church, the act of entering all that happens there. *Rinpoché* is a title given to highest respected lamas. The word means precious. *Lama* means mother. *Maha Kala* is Great Time. A *dorje* (or *vajra)* is like a sceptre or wand, the quintessential symbol of the "diamond vehicle" or Vajrayana Buddhist path. The vajra symbolises the immutable, indestructible state of Buddhanature. The *mantra*s are root sounds. So my dear audience here is my poetic description of the Maha Kala Puja.

CAGED MAHA KALA

MAHA KALA PUJA

Jan 29. Day one.
Small ceremony to receive blessing and enter Maha Kala mandala and be part of week-long puja. Maha Kala mantra given to all here.

Beginning of puja, new refuge, initiations. A friendly day of brother and sisterhood, food, walking around the stupa of Swayambhu, seeing the stupa in the sky. There it was floating on a cloud like seeing a spaceship. I turned in my westerner's shock, eyes bugging out, and asked another monk about it. He simply pointed at it and said, good luck for rest of great Maha Kala Puja. (Maha Kala, most wrathful deity, black in color.)

Day 2: Puja begins to boogie. Tibetan music the big horns the small, the chorus of voices. Then the Khenpo (translation: "the one who knows", the one who controls the magic) put the animal ignorance of a black dog inside a triangular box, we partook of a host which was Maha Kala. Also, part of puja was for Dorje Phagmo (vajrayogini), she yidam and he, Maha Kala the Dharmapala, our protector. (Before Puja began Satchyu Rinpoché, the headman of Swayambhu Gompa, came out for a pee and we had good vibe communication eye to eye.) Intense beginning, doors of temple closed for dog part of puja, monk assistants put red paint on paper. Finally one monk went outside to get dog, no dog would stay for ritual in temple, one monk put paper around dog, then Khenpo hopped on left leg, walked backwards into temple, aides wore cloth of yellow over mouths while aiding. When Karmapa prayer (he wasn't here but empty throne left for him) was recited, a dove landed on his throne and partook of some rice offerings. When door was opened a monk showed the dove out, then it flew clockwise around the stupa.

Day 3 night-time: A complete blackout in the temple for yab yum union of Maha Kala and consort done with power music and mantra; it went on for so long that time stopped and we all became in that union. This past afternoon we mellow from second day of half sleep. Puja becoming reality of creation. Khenpo making strong killing action with phurba and 10 implements. Slowly, slowly, mantras and horns, slowly killing ignorance of our minds, horns making strength in visualization more profound! A black cat appears under the Maha Kala head, black dogs look into the front door, butter lamps burning bright, perfection, oh so precious this juncture, my trust, more energy in consciousness (one pointed or remembering non-dual state).

Golden Beautiful Buddha
Golden Crown of Dhyani
Bow & Arrow Eyes Look Down from
Beyond on monks who sing
"death to our animal nature."

Caught in this thought,
My mind could scream in the darkness,
but the darkness is in whom I take refuge.

The Golden essence turns into
the Black one
and we monks
open what's called the mind
and pray to be kissed to the final death.

Tonight Satchyu Rinpoché is not downstairs with us, he's upstairs doing his own communications with deities. (His health is not good.) In this late late night not so intense, but then a great choir voice goes up, the drums beaten with the bow, beat a soft full time, the big Wheel of Dharma and OM MANI PADMI HUM wheels spinning the big drum low holy shacks lightly the walls, Maha Kala like the great conquering Zulu smiles from under his god's eye tent,

"may all beings be purified
in spite of themselves"

my dualistic eye spots the intestine fence and the trumpets
scream "RELEASE!
BECOME ONE WITH THE GREAT BLACK ONE,
HUNG!"

Let these lips and pen of mine only speak and write the truth unafraid.

End of late third night:

Refuge and 7-branch lamp prayers
Lineage Prayers

many offerings to converted demons of Maha Kala Mandala.
All visualize together to end third night, then common practices of each personal practice of individual monk and us the lay westerners.
Union!
Dam Zig (the kept connection with teachings, deity & Lama)

Day 4: As the beginning prayers roll out,
the Tea boys act silly and are beaten,
till more than enough,
and all of us in the temple are disciplined.
This thought rises,
"there is no one around to beat me,
so I suffer from my own ignorance,
more power rises in the atmosphere
some drums start slow
ascend
rise
come...

Hetty with a dream of skin & meat
I with eyes of dry flames see the puja
in deep wakefulness beyond this new life.
The puja a way of life.
400 days have passed.
Angus long on slow clarity, me...
the secret monk
longing to kiss the Dharmakaya.
More ignorance killed by the Khenpo.
Rinpoché sits on the throne, easy, pale,
with the sharpest damaru (drum) in town.

Night 4.

Other than having the thought "I don't know the way
to die"

I feel secure in
insecurity — oh oh ohh
christ...
oh oh ahh allah
oh oh ew ew oh ohh buddha

Gompa (temple)

sitting legs under
marching marching marching together
in mantra
yantra landscape
bleak
(piss break)
I could walk around the stupa
for years,
stopping for a moment to be fed,
home sweet home the lap of loving
kindness
Voidness

TORMA

Sleep night 4.

In the clear dawn with the skyline of fire and the horizon filled with snow cathedrals, monks speak of the whistle which we all could clearly hear, I thought it was produced along with rest of puja sounds, but now it is "a good sign, puja is going well." Maha Kala! 2 days ago also heard this sound.

Dream 2:

> The magic bird singing from on the stupa, everyone knows it is not a bird at all but something magic and the puja is being successful.
> The monks add mantra to the birds singing, but actually there is no bird to see on or around the stupa itself.
> The monks add mantra as we all walk around doing our om mani boogies. Our mantra becomes so loud that the bird's song disappears.
> The dream place changes and I am found painting a thangka (which I do in real life) and then many people from all parts of the world are painting in my house on Saraswati Hill, which is the left side of a saddle which holds Swayambhu Hill and Saraswati Hill. Hetty is there (she is the best painter, had shows in London before giving birth with Angus to first western child to become reborn high Rinpoche, discovered by no less than the Karmapa himself.) I'm talking to a fellow, handsome, and I feel jealous for some reason. I make his interest in what I'm saying come alive and then I ask him what he is feeling about me. Between my thumb and index finger is an insect like a giant centipede which can kill with a sting. I awake and know I am looking for someone to explore ha ah ha ha ha me and show me what I am. As this thought rolls out and I hear it I touch on the notation that I can only do this successfully by being a meditation. I shall sting myself. I the scorpio shall sting itself with anger for ignorance, sting itself into being an eagle then a phoenix.

Late Afternooon: Someone is on the Hill beating the big bell. Over and over in joyous abandon. There is a feeling of insanity and also a feeling saying "come Bhagwan come!". Many dogs begin to howl, the sound is hurting them somehow.

Day 5

In the fearful charnel ground of sandalwood
groves,
amidst the wisdom fire
treading on the opponents of the Dharma
Wonderful Maha Kala
His great and powerful voice
Fills the universe with the sound of
the Dharma
Arise from the natural clearness
DIspel the enemies of the Dharma
Within and Without
Great Maha Kala approach
Dark Maha Kala of great goodness approach
Great Guardian of the Dharma
approach.

(from Chompa
given to me by Hetty)

Night 5

The front door is like being pressed from the outside
by a great giant red balloon
under the door oozes some discursive thought
it is quickly swept away by chants,
the om mani padme wheel engine
slowly turns,
the drum,
the cymbal,
sweet full mantras
last of the …………
can't see an end
if all cancerous here
somewhere else other than Earth
the sweet sound of the Dharma will
be sung
and we like bumble bees
against the lotus flower
magnets
that know the absolute

Day 6

seat of enlightenment

throne of government

seat of speech

seat of inner voice

navel Heat center

root of all energy

Night 6

What is of value from this and this, is it the jumping up from bed, fully conscious of what is happening and continuing the active consciousness of preliminary practise? Waking up in the middle of the night!

Sunyata the clear mirror
&
Sunyata the clear reflection in the mirror
5 elements with the Body
Speech & Mind
in making offerings one knows the Sunyata
and tendril aspect in everything,

something is not one thing and known only as that
something is everything
and the void of self existing I,
I make puja
through the Sunyata Experience

Day 7 At first we see with our eyes, and desire arises
and then we want to feel it
and learn it
and be it
and transcend it

*

I got a mala in my bag
squeezing off the mantras
on the sneak

*

The Guru Rinpoché's
Mahamudra
come let's get it on!

giggle
slowly growing unattached
even unto death...

Night 7 With a lightness and almost rejoicing, the Marigpa
ignorance is thrown out the door, the horns blow in the temple
but come out directly from the Stupa,
marching, marching mantra
perfection,
Maha Kala
in the wisdom flames
AUM AH HUNG
BHAGWAN,
ignorance papers are cut into tiny pieces
and burned
then placed in the Black King's mouth,
red mouth, white teeth,
marchin, marchin
in lotus posture
AUM AH HUNG
DEATH, the death of ignorance!
rejoice!
rejoice!
rejoice!
BUDDHA, DHARMA, SANGHA,
OM AH HUNG

THE SENSES

BURNING KLESAS
or the shedding of our old skin of time

We all took a Light stroll
          from the gompa to the knoll
          all the monks in best dress
          the Rinpochés in red hats.

Lay tibetans and a tall lean poet
                    carried the head of Maha Kala
and a cage full of ignorance, down to its
                    burning ghat.

The man who's called "the one who knows"
          rang the dorje bell and pitched the garbage of a year
                    into a tent of hay,
his assistant added fire using match and kerosene,
          people
          rushed for a souvenir
                    a loose intestine
          one rupee   a piece of string,
          the monkeys in the trees,
                    the Maha trees,
          the Rinpochés,
          the drums, the horns like chandeliers
all screamed
"this is the ring of flames
                    for those who are alive,
throw the afterbirth under his black feet,
the feet of him the wisdom king will
step on it and grind it into gold"

          OH!
LEPERS WITH NO FINGERS GRAB for burning rupees,
children fight with nothing in mind but fighting,
a stranger from the west
with a mala on his wrist
          goofs,

"one can be amidst pure shit
and not be soiled."

The brown malignant stick flames slowly
turned to orange then light happiness,
folks still scrambled for a souvenir of ignorance

one Lama thought it funny
the other thought it natural, yawning
        "HO HUM   AH   OM
        OM AH HUNG,
        follow them all into their sleep Maha Kala
                                and awaken the BODHICHIT."

KHENPO WITH BELL

NEXT AFTERNOON AT ONE O'CLOCK

Afternoon during burning and night after burning

In front of the Gompa under the all-seeing eyes of Swayambhu, directly after burning (puja never ended down, during and returning) all monks performed music, light dance and continuing puja, many, many cymbals and symbols.

Around the box carrying the Maha Kala head Satchyu Rinpoché & Anzig Tulku with several other monks did more Maha Kala puja, slowly moving around the carriage which held the head, intestines, ignorance papers, plus money thrown in by regular folks of the community, Tibetan, Hindu, Newars, westerners. As they did the mantra with the music blowing heavy and beautiful, they stopped at the 4 directions. Much good open minded exchanging between all humans at this refined time on earth.

Everything burned as I explained in the Burning Klesas poem. As all the monks returned to the temple, tsampa (barley flour) was thrown by lay folk at each other, getting it on you is a great blessing. Obviously we were all covered with it especially we the westerners, as it is great fun to give us the best or worst of the deal. Hetty cut her leg trying to bestow much blessing back on the many. Satchyu Rinpoché said with a rather weird smile that "drawing blood after Maha Kala puja is good luck."

That night we saw specks of light glowing down in the burning place, a distinct glowing for sure. Today with 2 western monks who had noticed it also we saw again the glowing specks, Karma Lesche said "all day through the burning it was, emptiness is form, form is emptiness, emptiness is emptiness. The invisible Rinpoché is still sitting down there praying for the good luck and lack of more ignorance for his and all sentient beings, that is the glowing."

FORM IS EMPTINESS
EMPTINESS IS FORM

Same day after burning and the end of puja
the Khenpo's hands are shaking now from power
he sits in a chair in an open door
overlooking Kathmandu,
reciting magic over a fire,
making fire puja on the new year,
Satchyu does nothing
Tonight at 3 when the new moon
becomes
more blessing and puja, all the temple decorated
in the finest brocade, gold stitched dorjes & candy
fine tormas
offerings of the 5 skandas
5 deluded stains,
dogs barking, pen, everywhere I look there's a Buddha
surrounded by blessings
OM MUNI MUNI MAHA MUNI SOHA

NEW MOON — LOSAR — NEW YEAR
Be a rabbit who doesn't run away from a shadow

Gods are void, magic is afoot.

NEW YEAR'S DAY

Up to the magic stupa, blowing good wishes
                                        into the slot on the back wall
            of the Demchog Temple,
                        discussing with friends about the inside
                        chambers the one door and you enter
                        and there's 24 more doors
                                                only the right mantra
                                                lets you go into the
                                                middle of the mandala
up we go to Swayambhu
the big horns blowing strong and beyond long
and around we go
around the magic mantra tree the Buddhas
answer to space travel
the electric dynamo

the now familiar gompa door
            the dharma chakra above
and heavy purifying vibes within,

4 Rinpochés sit in a circle eye to eye in the 4 cardinal positions
and up we come a
            white kata in hand to get blessed
on the head by 4 gentlemen from
far Tibet

One feels like those paintings
of judgement day
the judges
the people in hell
all of them getting tortured bad by karmic hellkeepers
fallin
fallin
arms and legs and bare breasts
barbecued

the other way up golden stairs
with glowing faces
long white dresses
angels and whatever else
cooled out is happening in pure paradise

we all walk towards
openness the way to make offering
non-dual offerings
big smile,
your clarity is a blessing
Rinpoché.
thank you, thank you he says,
how are you?   he asks.
very good, very refined I say.

oh yeah   weeeeeeeeeee dutsie!

Each breath is Amrit
(on the morning of new year's day all Tibetan
folk believe that the first thing they see
or experience is an omen.)

the first thing the assistant monk saw was auspicious
(he told me of it) a full bucket of water,
a big wet omen.
the first thing I saw was a bare ass this morning,
bare and smiling with a funny grin,
I looked at it
with that old surprize,
I thought hoo-ray
let's spend a little more time in bed then time to
make it to the temple for some nectar
from the Rinpoché!

I withstood the cold
and the desert mouth
put on some clothes
and made my break to Swayambuooooo!
Oh Swayambhu

to be truly corny
is bliss
to kiss the hand that feeds you
down to the floor with
the humble knees
sweet spring of Dewa Chen
phospherescent rainbow from the
cord of the absolute
into me

Swayambhu
SwayambhuOOOOO
Oh Swayambhu …

NEW YEAR'S DAY, NIGHTLIGHT

On Tibetan New Year
            I'm down by the ashes
                        of the Maha Kala fire.
The glowing I saw the last 2 nights
            after the fire I think were pieces of the head

                        there are some teeth
                                    red lips
                                    an eyeball
                                                the bottom jaw
stares out still a beast
                        but dead
            the ignorance of the beast is dead.

I shan't walk into the ashes today
            they still have a powerful skull saying danger,

            skeletons can walk.

Crows are yet picking at the remains,
a pregnant bitch of a half breed jackal
                        looks for the 700th time for
                                    a tiny scrap she
                                    can put in her mouth,
            not me man I'm moving on
            unattached by the whole experience.

My neighbor plays an awful way out damaru
      and I'm slapping leather prostrations like a
fellow who knows why he's taking refuge.

SWAYAMBHU

MAHA-RISHI
MAHA-KARUNA
MAHA-BODHI
MAHA-MUDRA
MAHA-MAHA
HAHA-HAHA

VULTURE

WITNESS TO DEATH

Ashes to ashes, dust to dust,
when you die don't cling to your money belt.
Do not linger in the sobs of your loved ones,
if you do the wheel of ignorance is your only
home.
Death Death Death won't you spare me over
for another year.

Here today, gone tomorrow,
the face that I saw vomit and stop breathing
                    in the afternoon under
                    a tree, later that
night was a fiery figure in the middle of
                    drywood,
and this morn all that's left is campfire ashes
                    3 small bits of skull.
Death death oh death won't you spare me over for
                    another year.

It is easy to exist like monkey.
Jumping from tree to tree for tasty things.
Fighting over a peanut.

HEAVY MAGIC, A FOOT

"We are only taking the luxury of a peaceful
nuclear experience."
Inside the area around my shoulders
is a gorge, huge chasm receiving
some abstract conglomerations of distortions
. . . palpitations of paranoia.
A barbed wire mind.
Meanwhile down by the river that flows like a
stagnant puddle
there is 5000 pounds of bones,
the stage of Maha Kala the great destroyer.
He is dancing slowly, exactly on the
never ending delusions.
The foot steps and crushes and I become nothing,
NO THING.
Let the vision stay in your being till the conch
of freedom blows.
Take refuge in the essence of your mind.

DRAWING BY JEWELIE DEASY FOR THE POEM "ABSORBED"
IN *THE CLEARING STAGE*, BARDO MATRIX PRESS, KATHMANDU

ABSORBED

Absorbed into the home with 4 walls
the outside horns and voice calls,
learning what's new with the neighbors,
watching the neighboring farmers take in the harvest,
going to Bodnath and speak to the lamas.

5 hawks fly over Swayambhu Stupa,
the horizon is full of the highest white
mountains on earth, I stroll lightly
to Kathmandu, consciousness interested.

Snot noses, sidewalk shitters,
dried puja marigolds, goats and cows
for sidewalk partners,
Durga has gotten her blood,
Buddha's stone mudra means
it's a super illusion.
(please don't be affected by the crime of the rime)

Some poor buffalo has left his jacket on Pig Alley,
2 beggar serenaders sing under a window,
a stoned hippie with a *beti* and a green bottle
falls into the doorway of Uncle Tom's Cabin.

A japanese dude tokes and passes a chillum
over to an old saddhu,
Jimi Hendrix plays hard still,
those who missed Haight Street can do it
on Freak Street, get lessons for their future.

A cowboy with the face of a Nepali
asks me to change money
if he knew my condition
he'd know even the ink in my
tattoos is wearing out,
but with a quarter of India starving
beside me I smile at him and say no thank you.
My dog teacher passes with a torn rat in his
mouth, I know things can change quickly.

At the watery hole everyone stands clean
    in their Brahminy cords,
    a thousand years ago they accepted
    the populaton explosion.
Just seeing this is as satisfying as
    American Organic Health Food.
I go and pick up a letter at the Post Office
    from my parents, they say things are
    going strange there and money is the life blood of
    the nation,
    a dream comes and everything melts:

A white lady walks by with a Tibetan guy who
looks Italian, he's wearing coiled shoes and burgundy
robes, he screams at the top of his lungs,
"MEDITATION CAN BE FUN"
My hair is wild and long again!
I walk into an American library and scream
"Illegal aliens are destroying the jobless!"

        I am absorbed by the library
        people look up for one hairy moment
        then the whole thing becomes safe again.

        I wish I had three wishes
        if I had three wishes I'd wish for a glass of
        water 2 sleeping pills and a spanish girl
        I loved when I was seventeen,

        I'd tell her that ink blot (there on the desk)
        reminds me of you on a summer night at the beach
        your legs spread like seaweed
        and I eating you like you are totally everything
        good existing at once

        the waves keep beating us backward and forward
        and you hold my head tight to you.

LIVING IN THE PAST CAN BE TORTURE
LIVING IN THE FUTURE CAN CAUSE NIGHTMARES
LIVING IN THE NOW CAN BE THE MOST TERRIBLE DUE TO
the condition one is in at present . . . oh
I forgot where I was for a second,

DHARMA, CAUSE AND EFFECT
if you do everything for the sake of all life
you make no more bad effects
let's get on
with the trek

A LOVER'S POEM

My Buddhism and your beauty
weld me amongst disappearance acts
                                        and newspapers
            walking through walls
imagination is useless
where no habit patterns prevail

Ignorance speaks & Ignorance listens
HAHAhahahahahahahahaha

CLEAR DAY

like the seagull
            let your heart fly free
and like the sunset
let your heart glow
      with each breath I swear
            my love
      I never want control

like the creatures in the sea
swimming everywhere
I live to love you
      how easy life can be

one man's puja
    is
another man's cremation

alone in his bone home
    singing an om poem

at his home zone
out come a moan
moan

A SING ALONG SONG

Singing the Blind Man song
    No eyes seeing
    just working out on feeling
Eyes of White Light
    and Primordial sounds
Singing the blind man song
    no eyes seeing
    working out on feelings
eye of gold all gold
and a cold hard beat
    primordial sounds
Life energy like a snake biting
    its own tail
singing the blind man song
    eyes of white light
        primordial sound
nothing now but sounds
    fascination fascinated
hypnotized now now

KHAMTRUL & SATCHYU RINPOCHE

(at the saddle between Saraswati
and Swayambhu Hills)

Very real flesh
steps out of a yellow cab
in back of him 2
thin yogis
hair uncut
since maybe never.
The Rinpoché very big, looking about sees us
we are little children
he blesses us, lays a hand on our heads

we walk up the stairs
hearing him laugh, the word dorje on his lips.

There is a particular look to a Rinpoché's eye
a little off center
and not seeing the same as I.

He stops at the Demchog Temple to make short puja.
The air is filled with calmness.
Finished we stroll slow up to Swayambhu Stupa
where Satchyu Rinpoché meets him.
The small Satchyu
looks up into the face of the giant Khamtrul
and I feel
they are saying hello
as friends
from timeless years beyond,
they touch heads, this sparks
so much essence that emotion rises up
in me and I begin to slowly
cry.

They both turn the corner,
the Tibetan horns blow,
the air is filled with perfume,
everyone is as clear
          as water from a spring,
     all we
     friends united
stand at the manger
hands empty
minds full of gold blessings.

The two pros
walk
into the gompa.

left to right: SATCHYU RINPOCHE, DILGO KHENTSE RINPOCHE & assistant; *near wall*: ANZIG TULKU
foreground: KHENPO

RETURN (Kopan School, Kathmandu)

Well now we've met Lama Yeshe,
warmth, wisdom and compassion controller.
Again, this afternoon, our root basic sauce
for this course's enlightenment,
Lama Thubten Zopa Rinpoché.
As Lama Yeshe is the father,
Lama Zopa is the brain child.
Hmmm, Yah, from the Holy Teachings of
the Great Bodhisattva Dalai Lama,
"Those who desire to benefit
sentient beings by their compassion
for all beings will discover in checking up,
that it is the Bodhicitta that is best.
Also person not practicing is very foolish.
It is like a person who arrives in jewel land
by good luck
but leaves from jewel land empty handed."

SARASWATI breakage wakeup

Blessed Breakage
Season Change on the Horizon
There is fresh white snow on the mts.
A new voice is in the sparrow
A robust rooster
A chill to wake up to . . .
    jump up in
        and sit in lotus

The Sun of Dawn breaks molten
Jagged clouds stand frozen
Seasons change cuts across the eyeballs

PRAYER TO NEPALI PRIMORDIAL ARTIST

Wisps of mist
    Hang connected to the River
                        by a string
Raindrops drip green drips
        clean from the Leaves of Trees
What could be so
                    great
    as the living on Manjusri & Saraswati Hill
        and looking out the window at Swayambhu?

At the end At the Place At the Range
            where vision ends
        mountains line the lower sky
        in bumps and bows in peaks

                    and flows like the finest
                        lines ever made in ink.
Great fruit Bats flap a sound of leather,
        the stupa to Swayambhu
shines outward in the Valley filled with
        Temples.

Monkeys walk the roofs,
Tibetan horns, Newarie Drums,
Red and Green Water Jewels twinkle in the
Morning Rays of the sun
As the Rain Clouds Scatter in Silent
Explosions
Water Getter's Gather at the Well
speaking in 4 different languages

Everyday a different pattern
some change in the mode of the
Primordial Artist.

MANJUSRI

HOOKED TWISTED WAKING

Monsoons gone
this flicker of autumn
can't hold its name
against the cold Himal Wind
Certainly I have been changed from
last Spring
Vandalized by Surrealism
so sweet their twisted images

Hooked on Echoes of my own past
like these winter damp clouds
which cover the things that Summer
has done
In the dawn's mist old things wake
and a frost kills the fresh grass
By the time the sun has broken the
cold
I am living my role of yesterday

IRA COHEN AND PETRA VOGT PHOTOGRAPHER UNKNOWN

SMALL DELUSION ON A BIG ILLUSION

I'M GOING BACK WITH A LINGAM
        FOR ACHILLES' GRAVE
AND IN BABYLON DRY I SHALL
SEARCH FOR CYRUS'S EAR
THEN TO PLACE IT LIKE A COUCH
AND WAIT FOR ALEXANDER'S
SPEECH ON IMMORTALITY,
YES, HIS TEN INDIAN HOLY MEN ARE GONE
FINALLY DEAD FROM WRONG ANSWERS

I HAVE BEEN SLEEPING WITH THE ILIAD
        NEXT TO ME
I HAVE BEEN KEEPING MY PROMISE
  OF SENDING STRANGE CREATURES
    BACK TO MY FATHER
I APOLOGIZE IF THEY ARE NOW ONLY
    PHOTOS

GIVE ME SEVERAL MADMEN
    TWO FLIPOUTS AND SEVEN EXILED
        NEW YORKERS
I CARE TO FUCK THE WORLD
I LONG FOR POLITICAL POWER

IN THE BODH GAYA MANDALA

So easy to just sit down for a moment
    and OM MANI PADME HUM ____________
    ROUND AND ROUND & round we go _______.
If I desire I'd leave desire right?
                                        haven't I got that power huh?
haven't I the power somewhere to decide whether
                                                  om mani padme hum
          I can find meaning in all the words behind
                                                  om mani padme hum
                                                                  it all.

All this that stretches out in front
                                        in back
                              around the side
    circumambulating from one maze
                                        to another
                                        without finding out
                                        the center
                                        was inside
    all this circumambulating around
                                                  myself

Om mani padme hum
around the Xmas tree ever since
I was born
          add a little tinsel
                                        here
a little tinsel
there
and when you're pinned again
                                              in
          that formulated game
put a star on top and grade it
A, B, or C
          and the bottom will drop out
          and I will die again

Life _________The Pursuit
Apathy
Browbeat Dog Tired
Nervous
Imbalance
Disease sick
Sicker
Sickest
Dead
Afraid---------------------------
Lost
Beyond even That
Grasping with no Hands
Screaming with no Mouth
Craving and grasping and
becoming
AHH sigh of relief
LIFE
THE PURSUIT BROWBEAT
DOG TIRED
NERVOUS
IMBALANCE SICK
SICKER

HAPPY DHARMA JINGLE

Oh Joy, joy for 1 more day,
to have the strength to practice the way,
As the opened eyes view the morning light,
the beginningless curse again trips to arise.
I prostrate to the wisdom jewel,
good morning impermanent world.
Oh Joy, joy, joy for the precious chance
to enlighten myself
and all sentient life.

OH!
OM MANI PADMI HUM

DEAF AND DUMB TIBETAN WOMAN

COMING DOWN TO CIVILIZATION
AFTER 3 MONTHS IN THE HIMALAYAS
WALKING BACK DOWN TO KATMANDU

Is that a human being up there?
A female . . . rotted hair
    sitting dazed in the sun,
in a filthy town,
stagnant people chasing bald-headed chickens,
    enjoying the joy of throwing stones at birds?

Namaste!   Cigarette?
Coming down to Civilization,
the place of filth where you find the people.
How can I help these sorry bastards
or stop a giggle at passing a blond boy
    in a St. Pope Paul Christian T-shirt?

        Coming into Civilization
            mind burning
        Civil-Lie-Zation
        I feel like a Confederate
        after the Civil War!
        Coming down, down, to Civilization
            waterfalls with barking dogs!

I can feel the magic radios again on the footpath
close to the highway, the radio wave jib-blah-wish
    a lady in a sari closing in.
Katmandu the temple in the toilet
    coming to you
from the humbling white mountains.
Was that a Mickey Mouse canteen I saw back there?
Mind flayed! passing a Japanese Jewish boy with
an Indian child with horn rim glasses behind
him a neanderthal with a blunt ax, he throws me
a kiss chirping like a brazen queer on a corner
of america . . . a portrait in surreal.

Come to Himali land and see primates, mother nature
reaches deep in to present her last treasures.
Hey baby let's smoke a joint and take the tram to
Everest.   Choking . . . porters carry things in
CuttySark boxes, Namaste! Bless your young dehydrated
cunt Namaste from gurung cave man with a TWA
travel bag, Namaste from Dorje Chang blue sky
and a trace still of white peak skyline,
            shoes disintegrating
            knees disintegrating
            friends disintegrating
            scheduled meditation times disintegrating

            me and my love
            sit in lotus as the guru friend
            who got information from a guru
who read *Meditation In Action* and visited Bodh Gaya
saw the Dalai Lama in Stockholm got fucked up the
ass by a monk got enlightened by injection
and we come closer.
Ramche, small hill town, restaurant full
of healthy bodies with the eyes of the dead staring out
only desire in starched collar and bare feet,
they have seen *Playboy*
they have been cursed by moslem-hinduism combo
and I'm stoned again on a death-trip,
a self-styled Staten Island Buddhist.
I prostrate to those who are not Lamas coming down.
I prostrate to the cook she is sweet happy we like her food,
coming, blue clouds floating over border tribes with shovels
and picks fixing the footpaths to the Himalayas.
There's a Japanese Miss snapping flicks
she has me in the background getting rupees from my orange
backpack, I pose, behind me white peaks shine light years
away the Chenrezi cave we made for
            eyes bright, the poet,
                        his consort,
      Dharma words,
            the Bodhisattva is back there in essence, we
are here watching the miles clockwatch dogma
budding Bodhisattva baloney coming down a regular
vague haze . . .

what i remember most is I'm selfish,
and one night in the full moonlight
the ghost white mountains were too
powerful to look at and I was humbled
for a moment for the first time.
Into the last dribbles now.
Lang Tang, Gosainkunda, Helumbu BE DO BE
Lang Tang, Gosainkunda, Helumbu BE DO BE DO
please don't let me hold a grudge on the 20th century

must break the curse of take
lalala lalallalalla la la la
so much and we're so mundane
and if I don't copy this pencil into ink
it'll all rub off the page.

We pass a pipe made from a leaf, and smoke a poor
man's tobacco and smell (our dying sense of smell)
rice paddies, dinosaur buffalo
with baby-faced calves,
the distant Himal Ganesh.
A fella with a Karmapa black hat button
flirts with my gal, everything perfect
in the cosmic plan,
I admit no understand,
dribble, don't feel brave in admitting the
dull words dripping down
towards Civilization.
The river picks up more
water, getting warmer like blood
more stuff,
it is easy to have excuses for your own negativities
Justification
Rationalization,
a skinny little man stops
and sits sobbing about the walk up and the hot.
His eyes are deep down and I give him a candy
and I give him a problem
he doesn't know what to do with it,
ahh, that little man,
he'll save it for his
grandchild later.

BY THE HOLY RIVER GANGA

Death is floating in the river, calmly floating
downstream.
Once a vessel for a consciousness to flow in,
now a pleasure island for a vulture with all
the accommodations of the Hilton.
Slowly floating down the Ganges on a Sunday
Afternoon.

DIGESTION

Unattached, unattached, renounce, renounce,
                    suffer now instead of later,
                    suffer with joy with Bodhicitta.
The hells are full of ones who've never learned
                    it, for years they search the land for
                    water when the Dharma would quench their
                    thirst in one moment.
So solid is my reality, hard rock is hard,
                    tree bark real as my body,
     why not a more horrible reality later caused by
                    all my negative Karma.
Death, damnation, hellfire, especially now that
     someone else has told me the answer . . .
                    "Buddha, Dharma, Sangha" (3 screams
                                        to wake us)
     Someone has snatched my ignorance away, stolen the
     landscape.
     My theories are going down the river backwards.

MONKEYS FALL LIKE STONES

MONKEYS fall like stones
    down Swayambhu Hill,
almost all day long I've heard you chant,
    "OM MANI PADME HUM"
so you were all very surprized when
    I picked the pretty puppy up
    rubbed its face on a statue of Akshobya
    and smashed its head into soft blood
    against the Dhyani Crown of Ratnasambhava.

All day long monkeys fall like stones from trees
        on Swayambhu Hill.

Monkeys jump from stupa to stupa, eating the offerings
        made to the Buddhas,
    in animal joy they leap,
    concentrated ghoul eyes bugging out,
their cute antics show me the similarity between me
    and them,
    very close
    the contrast,
  everything mostly on the surface.

A monkey takes a dive from Amitabha's samadi hands
        and lands
breaking the link that makes him a metal man
no more afraid to manifest any sensitivity
            in front of anyone
beginning to part from the hairy ape sangha,
laughing in earnest!
A typhoon cyclone blows objects into strange positions,
        the full moon is ripe!
                NOW WHAT!

Monkeys falling like rain, grabbing popcorn
in both hands,
never a delightful savior, too fast the competition.
Monkeys fall like stones
into the loving cup of Vairacana
become Path Apes
Sun Lovers
Void Freaks
True Motherfuckers!
All that's left is the Naga King Amogasiddhi
up the spine
and into the land of the furtherest
most west.

FIVE DHYANI BUDDHAS

OM	HUNG	SWA	AHM	HA

seed of 5 male families

MUM	LAM	MAM	PAM	TAM

seed of 5 female families

HOLI

Nearly savage, dancing wild & loose
and gesturing to the sky
with fanatic sound,
clattering cymbals,
the men's faces covered in
phosphorescent red powder
celebrating Holi,
screaming at the top of their voices
reveling in some strange brotherhood

tourists file quickly down into a waiting bus,
none dare point a camera in
the screaming procession's direction
ages crash together with no desire
for intimate relations

looking to the horizon
snow castles stand like the best of visions,
rock, sky, cotton-candy, mountains

the air is filled with banging drums, hand cymbals,
and screaming

full moon march first hindu holi day

FIRE PUJA

MORNING OF THE VIRGIN STUPA

Life sometimes moves into a quick leap
and maybe maybe becomes one virgin stupa
alone and venerated by dancing madman
some pastel glow felt from the move metamorphosis

so rare is it that even a cliff
must have the courage to jump,
to be thrown by a monster is perfect
especially if it whispers at the push
"there is no bottom"

white mother stupa
golden father stupa
one virgin stupa screaming in the evening
of existence

falling spinning in the ever confusion of the push
passing through everything with interest
but not grasping for a saving memory
which would save this life but ruin the
fall

LAMA MEANS MOTHER

Being in the light of a nice,
        enlightened man,
        and him a teacher,
        what a blessing.
A helping hand the biggest helping hand
        a person can give.
A hand that pulls you out of suffering
    by showing you a way you can perform
                                yourself.
And telling you to keep Working, keep working.
    And don't forget to say, "May all Beings
                                        Be Happy.

P.S.   write me a letter
        and tell me how
        you're doing.

THE YOUNG TANTRAS

Beings that I been in the good and bad mandala
        since this form of suffering began,
and now,
        even though I'm sitting on the back of the
        roaring snow lion,
        just before the throne of the Buddhas,
in the very midst,
        I fear the loss of this position
        I grasp for the teachings that are
            being freely given,
still within are the habits of an ignorant bastard,
still thinking
I need a mother and a father
and many types of communication.

this year's goal is Buddha's Vajra
travel into made worlds
        visualizing outrageous symbols
        forgetting,
        scratching my head in open space,
intensely curious . . .

in the market place fruit and vegetables
are being sold
on the scene the styles circle
one could discuss something and watch buttocks
    in the evening as the sun sets, all the way
    until death,
    my skin isn't as fresh
    10 sperm spurts later
    and my love is still the same.

won't you cuddle my bliss baby?
        Because it is only one half grown you can't
        accept it.
We've been so far away from each other and there has
        been no way to exchange hellos.
I carry you to bed in my shallow dreams.
I carry it to bed in my shallow dreams and rise with
a mantra on my dry lips
to cut the bliss baby umbilical cord
when it is not yet quite awake.

TARA

THE MTS.

Mountains have with them
        a hunchback's torture
    the roar of a lion
        the slope of its shoulder

they look like the sound of waves
    a laughing lake of hunchback mazes

    I know there lives inside these castles
        the rainbow makers
                of the inner (heat) warmth
            they are THERE
                LAUGHING LOUDER BEHIND the SNOW
                    AS THE COLDNESS GROWS

    PINK DRAGONS IN PURPLE FLOWERS
    fly to the music of the glacier drops

        another
        lavender phoenix dives
            into the pale blue shadows
                a murder of crows rides on his
red feathered shoulders

        their voices look like
        thin icicles on rock

in the hot blue river
  each lip of the sherpa
    is cold in their hovel
each word from a new-born child
    is cause for smiling

every breath is the good
                of the lung
    every drink pure
                blood
        of HIMAL

DORJE CHOPPER
(KNIFE OF THE DAKNIS)

MASSES PASSES SIDEWAYS

A swirling mass

all so sure of the next meal
sure its got to come or death will come…
a swirling mass
jelly like proto-zoids
leather skinned pachyderms
pink soft humanoids all hungry and quickly
frightened by anything
that slightly seems to carry pain.
Endless funnel (horn-like unicorn)
of hungry always beasts with burdens
their in control is out of control
swirling in a mass of pursuit and retreat
the odors appalling.

Religious banners die hard eyes
getting the holy consecration
only at the hour when talking the dogma
into others, drugged on morphines and metallic
cocaine in the same manner it all helps to
loosen their lips and Frenchy can walk
in the street at noon and not scream madness
at his reflection in the barbershop window!
Group back slap,
Harmonious Energy Pickpockets.

The pursuit mirage,
brick upon brick of intellect
away from groundings.
Cement of yes nods and exchange
of common courtesies
little hints that something
can be accomplished together.

Everywhere my eye connects there is intercourse,
even when there is fucking others hardly can
wait for the other to finish,
so much stress is laid on getting inside
and after 5 minutes they lay exhausted,
one dwarf spent 10 years thinking
of some Ramona,
for a brief moment he saw her
through a keyhole he saw her
he dropped his life's blood on the
door panel.

Everywhere my eye connects there is trying
and crying for perfection,
most of those only reach
being wary,
with police dogs on their doorstep while
inside they slowly
withdraw from their
initial attraction.

Who's got the power to turn off da machine?
Who's got the power to turn off the tape recorder?
You so freshly tell me of your dreams
but what about your real!
The tell-tale trance of longing, of grief
of knowing we're nothing more or less
than this odor under perfume over.

My scar is open
or is it still open
and running with filth...
hare, hare, I laugh with the rocks,
a tourist with no visa
to anyplace lasting

BABS' Baby JUNIPER

(death of a friend's 4 month old child,
written at the burning ghat)

There is a growling thunder around,
the eminence of a personal death is in the air.
Can you stand the pain of someone you love dying?
Tell me if you can stand in the rain and not
get wet.

So beautiful the day.
Are you still here in your body?
So slight you are, I know you could disappear,
go back between an inhale and an exhale,
all the way back to another condition.
Your suit of clothes hardly worn.
No one will get to know you because
when getting home the mass is going on.
I can't judge whether to be sad or glad
that the newborn baby is gone.

They'll need so little wood
and just a little fire,
hardly any smoke you'll make today,
down by the river.

TARA GIVING BLESSINGS

BOUDHANATH

this island
Buddha Boudhanath
saffron thrown
of om mani padmi
round & round
this circle
this circle
for offering
this island
whiteness
surrounded
by puja
simple surrender

this island
saffron thrown
this island
om mani padmi hum
om mani padmi hum
of symbols
of dialogue stopping
up dialogue
of whiteness
blackness
surrounded
prostrations

the KALI SONG

Fiery flames, stretched across the
universe
who is that black dame dancing with
her sword out?

Time is her name
destruction is her game

Kali does the dance, the dance of destruction,
time is her name,
she does the dance of heat
burning burning burning
Kali does the dance the dance of destruction,
nothing to do but sit down
or dance with her in illusion
she does the dance of heat,
Shakti energy,
burning burning burning
burning burning burning
burning burning burning.

PROSTRATION

RATTLE ON

Rattle on, rattle trap brain
Cause I'm a liberation soldier gonna put you down
Here and now with pure love is my aim,
No more self torture in a beginningless game.
Rattle on, rattle on, putting purification oil
on the wheel,
slipping away from these old ideals.
This outside me has so many things.
But this inside place has only me talking to myself.
There must be more than this talk.
I'm sure the inside path leads to the absolute truth.

Little Robert Francis
is getting tired of all the dances,
to awake the sleeping Buddha would be much better.
Happy BIrthday Baby you're one more year closer to the cemetery,
best press your salvation accelerator.
There's a trillion *me*s like me
and we pray to one thing or another,
well I got this little will power
so I'm gonna listen to the rattle,
but in remaining solid the rattle will pass
on to another rattle
so rattle on till all your
rattling ways are gone.

TREK TO LANG TANG MOUNTAIN AND BACK
(20 THOUSAND FEET)

AMIDST AMONG TUMUNG
SHERPA GURUNG
SWEET BREEZE

A SONG

WE GO TO
LANG TANG, GOSAINKUNDA HELUMBU BE DO BE
I'm up the river, and through the woods
trekking into the core of good
going to
Lang Tang, Gosaikunda, Helembu (3 times)

I do perceive that I see a snow peak
crystal ice palace, eternal whiteness
oh moving up to
Lang Tang, Gosaikunda, Helembu be do be

Gor-ra tabell (moist slower sweet)
Gor or ra tabell
Gor-ra -to bell lalala Om -----

each breath is amrit
sweet as an angel's kiss
Om Ah Hung
I visualize the essence of my mind
bejeweled and blue skin sitting in splendor
I surrender!
on our way to
Lang Tang, Gosaikunda, Helembu ooooooh

p.s. the only way to dance with the the high snow peaks is to surrender and in the process the sweet view will bless you.

THE DAYS BEFORE MEETING THE KARMAPA

My designs are not the usual ways
            of meeting the Karmapa
    in these days before his coming
    I go further
leaving the valley of the temples
for the lower lands of Pokhara.
Each revolution of wheels
brings in the picture more clear
        as to my position
        on the battlefields
        between the making of a
        pure mind
        and my ever present
        forces of ignorance.
Following the river out on this
        injured bus
    all things are beauty full
    but it comes to me as I linger
    an odor of the burning ghat
        that snaps a laugh in two
    exploding pictures on the darkness side
            of closed eyes.

Inside
"we both lay eyes on each other
only the eyes for the other
                exist for the other
then the feeling in me feels a natural
            expansion
        like a visit from a lover
and I have finally seen the Karmapa
            in the flesh."

In my waking day
        I'm tasting yellow brown
            paranoia again,
    it seems like some plan that's not my own
        as I move further away
            across the holy land of Nepal
away from what seems to me
    my life's crowning experience.

WILL YOU BE MY SWEETHEART?
(a Karmapa Visit)

The earliest morning people are Chinese,
fully uniformed in blue with small hats
and bags of corn,
feeding the monkeys by the holy steps that
Karmapa will walk by hours from now.
All kinds of folk are floating about,
strangers to the hill,
he will organically come
when the moon is a full magnet.

The day the Karmapa came monks rode motorcycles,
beginners fell to their knees
and knew the reason why they did it.
As children adults drew chakra pictures all over
the ground, a person who can go to any
heaven or hell will cruise through all of
our prostrations.
(i can hardly make myself tell you about the
black hat ceremony)

The day the Karmapa came commercials from India
raved about hair oil and this prayer poem rang of Walt Disney
from a life of Mickey Mouse being a Tutelary Deity.

I am so happy to be here for the coming of Karmapa,
happy cause I will be able to see him,
everyone has their amount of sincerity
towards a saint
(easy to think he ain't)
who has kept up the vigilance
until his mind is clear of all
conceptions
who has done the supreme inner and outer
yogas
until there are no obstructions
and now
his essence speaks "try and it will
be yours."

Mind like the sky
Sky Mind
the needed strength to endure the more than
countable eons
of ignorant self-destructive beings.

Karmapa is coming,
the victory banners and parasols of energy,
emotion pulling back the tears of Joy,
"the sakti mother has room to bless everyone,
the combination of prayer and upaya keeps him here
to keep the wheel turning."

Satchyu Rinpoche the elder abbot of Swayambhu
says to no one around but me,
"the Karmapa is coming."

Now in a turn of time
a wind shield with one large grin
came around the curve and up the hill,
the face of Chenrezig appeared
and was Karmapa.

Then he was walking (with everyone). i never noticed
if he moved his legs
and all the kinds of devotion screamed up the street
and up to the stupa, he disappeared into the gompa
leaving
the sunset and some golden specks moving amongst the air.

The day the Karmapa came was Valentine's Day, a big
red heart with an arrow through it,
and everywhere from now it is easy to see his face
on the top of my head.

OM AH HUNG.

THE BLACK HAT MAN

IN POKHARA
SEX WONG (puja) OF AMITAYUS
good rushing river the strange color
        of milk
    above the eternal white
        snow mountains
        with that postcard stillness
    the black hat is taken out
        of its flowering brocade
            hat box
        a translucent gem on top with
        jewels everywhere and
            a crystal mala
        slowly fingered in deep samadhi
3 times the ceremony and at
    the end a stupid near
        riot to receive
            a lovely blissful
blessing from his HOLINESS KARMAPA

KALU RINPOCHE RECEIVING BLESSING FROM KARMAPA   PHOTO BY NOEL COBB

KARMAPA'S AMITAYUS WONG IN POKHARA

THE SECOND ARRIVAL OF KARMAPA

(sitting in the highway dust, vultures over head)

waiting by the side of the road again
behind me & to the side
the snow mountains will be the
        backdrop for your face
I truly don't have anything better to do
        but wait for you
to see your happy smile
    to hear your charming voice
From here the road stretches back
        to Kathmandu
    where thousands have been
            blessed by your wongs.
once again I wait for your
    laughing jeep
    to putt putt bom bang into view.
I want to watch again your special
    trick, the black hat number where
all the different realms open up
and breathe while you smile and turn
    the dharma wheel.

P.S.   how's this for an inside joke:
    for hermits lice are pearls of
    god. If that's true I am an
    oyster bed on a landlocked
    ocean.

SURREAL LAMA

RETREAT 33 (on Kim Dole Hill)

Swayambhu golden blasts in the evening
with Tibetan blessings,
Nepalis and Newaris picnic
while Karmapa's sky mind
says hello to this clear-aired
Himalayan Valley:

look out for what's coming
it is darkness ascending from India
in the form of joyful excited people
my light shall retreat to security
a security that follows a natural law
and helps in my not exhausting my forces.

Not in the forms not in the thoughts
not picturing the pictures of any devil to fly from
just knowing my limits
not forgetting the goal
I wave good-bye to you for a while
for I am in trouble and shall not become undone.

II

May love be with you & me
as we struggle our vital energies
thinking our luck will change.
May you survive
while my neck bedecked by a yelllow cord given
me by the Karmapa signals retreat
and refueling of primordial strength.
Let's be friends if friends we have become
in these days full of power and wonder
I purpose a merger of great thought
and everything filled with voidness
we inferior climbers are the heroes
of the Kali Yuga.

III

the great man has been seen
and vows of liberation taken
certain laws protect one from evil
knowing well I am not a great swimmer
I will not at this time
attempt to cross the great water
        I surrender
        and retreat from this
        tiresome conflict
                between me
                and myself

KING of YAK

Then I saw the king in the stone corral,
    sniffing at a spotted cow,
    he got up on her, all his
    wonderful fur feathers flying loud.
As he walked along alone
    all else moved in the necessary
    pattern he was inventing.
He squatted like a dog, he lifted up
    his huge earth colored tail,
    he shit yak shit
    the color of autumn.

Buckskin Brown Bull is him
    the center of the yak mandala.
Big Bull Yak whose shade trees
    are the Himalayas.

HIMALAYAN CONDOR

Rock & Roll condor
    gliding in fury over the mountains
        pointed glacier eyes dancing
        a cold view looking down
                for something rough & raw
            a hard blue sky
            with his screaming curve of
                feathered wing
                above the rocky lines
        there flies the king of the airs.

THE BLOODY KILLING POLE

SLOW

The young bull buffalo is tripped to the
stone ground in front of the
Ganesh Temple,
its feet pairs, front and back are tied together
then the 4 legs tied together,
his body is pulled into facing the image
then the head is pulled back tight
against the body and tied with rope
to the legs,
this tightens the neck, exposing the vein,

water is poured on its body and head,
orange tiki powder put on the horns,
rice, flowers and other offerings
are thrown on the head,
his body is pulled closer to the image.

A man with a sharp butcher knife
slices open the thick skin
and opens it up exposing the fat tissue

he then cuts through the fat tissue
exposing the red bloody flesh,
cutting down more he reaches the
jugular vein, he cuts a cord
and ties it around the jugular which is
shining in the sun,
the bull's eyes are wide open but glazed.

Pricking the large vein the man aims the
pulsing out blood at the image
the blood hits the image directly
coating the bronze in red wash
while others do puja around the image.
The man cuts slowly the head completely
away from the body
and it is laid at the feet of Ganesh,
the body like a wet rag
lays in a thick purple
puddle of blood
as people walk by on their way everywhere.

THAT MAGIC

Slight Breezes Blow over Erections.
Cotton Blue Blouses lay bare the Long Horizon.
Upside Down Bowling pins, thighs of yellow gold,
it is Harvest Time in the Spring,
a young man's fancy dances.
How much beautiful Beautiful is in anything?
A little conversation, to touch warm
elements.
To Breathe it in and breathe it out, and crash together,
Floating,   Burning,   Flying,   Solid.

RAINY DAY (DAY of SUMMER SOLSTICE)

sitting in an atmosphere moist
    whether weather is real or not
    sitting talking in an ambrosia bath.
thought pictures move in & out
    a justified sound of rain when in
a house,
a dripping roof.

RAINBOW
BLOOD SOUND
BUBBLES RISING
the SOUND OF A SINGER
IN THE CRYSALIS OF MY TUNE
SARASWATI SWEET GODDESS
OF MUSIC
YOUR BLESSING FELT
ECSTATIC
SURRENDER
MOVE
LOTUS PETAL RAIN
SARASWATI, SWEET GODDESS OF LEARNING
VIBRATING THE FIBERS OF BEING
CURRENTS OF WISDOM
like the pitter patter of atoms
sitting all this happening
but relaxed ---------------
must be simply the right time
the right place
for living a life that is only fiction
on most parts of the planet:
no longer a teen with the screaming question
now I hold the TOUCH OF CERTAINTY WRITTEN BY
A GENTLEMAN NAMED JAMGON KONGTRUL PLUS A
GENTLEMAN I MET DOWNTOWN IN
Bodhgaya he was being Chenrezig at the time
but went by his own name now and then also
it was Kalu Rinpoché a true saint if that term
fits these days, anyway when it came to knowledge
and compassion he was the divine example of that
embodiment.

OLD HUT LIFE

The shadow of a crow
  winds its way like a snake
    across the yellow sand
light specks shoot into this palm
    branch hut
  the wind shakes it
the light becomes moving diamonds
      across the dry leaves

conjuring for the word (weird)
  in a heavy strong blow
the land covered in wind voice
  whose tension personality
    is now peaking

she was flipping out in the corner
  into a glass beer mug
grunt noises cut the endless wind play

  don't leper me
  mother nature
your veins of blue give blessing today
    hopefully . . . .
the sneak thief death knocks on my
  cotton door . . . no noise, no answer

for there
is
NO DEATH TEACHINGS
TO THOSE WHO HAVE
NEVER HEARD
OF THEM
NO DEATH TEACHINGS
AND A CURSE
TO THOSE WHO
HAVE HEARD OF THEM
and not
attempted their practice

SCORPION PROTECTOR

THUNDERBOLTS stand FLOWING

If it be false that conscious awareness
while experimenting with
positive and negative
action
rids it all by thunderbolts (vajra)
then surely I make ready for the
grim curse.

Having the most beneficial of locations on earth
on top with meditation experts near to the
light house for the direction of darshan
and clouds
to the flowing down realms of
suffering of the malignant wish
to be something other than a tool
of motion within screaming creaming beings
not flowing.

God the cricket's click splits my
sections of brain,
their sound is a mad castinet
played by cameo midgets.
Each hit of the stick against the back
of a cow reminds me of how easy it is
to suffer inside this
skin of cardboard
and Ah
if I were interrupted in these rainbow spaces
by the owners of this country I'd be on fire
down to the border into the nether world
where each second can be a fearfilled death
and loss of identity.

Oh shroud me in your golden invisible,
each sun is warm and this is where my brain
feels comfort

how can I be
the smiling yes man whose compassion game
is the official joke in the rooms of
just about everybody.

This earth is the place of tokens and get well
cards, pay toilets grab my flesh and pull
baby in.
I am condemned never to piss for free.
What is lovely tortures me into their
turning ugly.
Must I sit in quietude and wait just
wait for the end that doesn't exist . . .

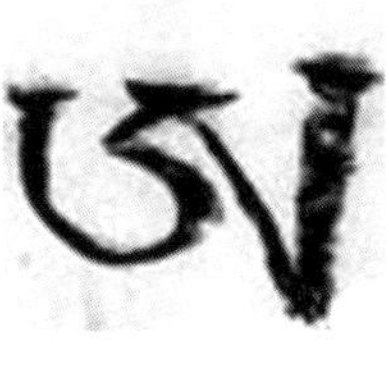

DHARMADHATU BIRD

DHARMADHATU BIRD

All winter long I longed for the song
of the cuckoo hoopo bird,
today it has returned,
on the day of the new moon.
It warbles of the Dharmadhatu.
Its throat blows out like a bubble
and quivers out like moving Jell-o tones
so fine they crack the landscape into
the excellent clarity
of the high god realms

hoop woop hoop woop
woop woop woop woop
everything stops and listens
hoop hoop hoop hoop
what does it mean by its singing
woop woop hoop hoop
on the hills of Saraswati & Swayambhu
overlooking all the valley
woop woop hoop woop
(BUDDHA, DHARMA, SANGHA)

CHINESE NIGHTMARE

Automatic weapons with young boys
    fingers twitching on their triggers,
        the bullets making quick dust clouds
            on the Hill.
Following along the weapon's gunsight the
bullet runs across a greenfield, hits
onto a brown hill, beyond is a larger hill
which climbs up to the great stupa, Swayambhu.
The all-seeing eyes look down on the troops
in army green and Kathmandu City.
King Whatever-his-name is the living manifestation
of Vishnu the Preserver.
Buddha, the awakened one,
blesses the warrior slaves of China,
while I sit idly masturbating another day away.

IN THE BLOOD COVERAGE

A Carnival around the body
of a young buffalo,
cameras snapping as the spirit screams
in fright
in pain
the best shots are when the body lays like rubber
and the neck
drips red
oh bread and butter
next comes the sweet young
goat
the door of the temple is burnt scarlet with blood
Kali energy there for real

this young buck
in the face of that door
gets a screaming hard-on
a pounding inside his hard cock is pounding
the potion
of adrenalin and kundalini
2 realms at once making love
give this goat supreme majestic
energy
and at that minute
its throat is cut
the blood splashing against the door frame
a useless figure flopping on the concrete
steel hard knife cutting bone
primordial gallow with guillotine
a pain so cold
the head removed and laid on the doorstep
long seconds ago it was already accepted by the
union and the added power of
death

My mala snaps in my hands
beads bouncing into pieces of diamond
in the sunlight
my mantra screams into
movement
blood everywhere
crunching of bone
my own
death
fantastic!

The mouth of the goat
showing teeth that smile
out of puckered lips
that kiss at the Yum
(lips of Kali)

A UNIVERSAL CHILD, the TOWN CRYER

I mourn the essence of Buddha
caught between the Chinese communists,
the Indian Red Necks
and the seasoned protectors, the
humble red cross.
The subtle slow system drags closer and
closer to the time that no one will care that
they are bound by greed and that it's better to be
a humble worker than a caring human.
(survival aah!)

I mourn dirty tea house tea, filth causing
disease . . . dirty kids holding catapults killing
little creatures or the big boys doin the army
way of Coca Cola hoooooray!
Progress is our most important product, to get
the poor to school you have to sacrifice down home
mother earth.
A week ago I overheard that a bad omen has been
created.
The highway to Old Peking destroyed a Naga Pond
in the back of Swayambhu's hill.
It is all too real, history in the making.
Blind greed making lusty decision.
Another medal of honor, a suit of pure gold
for the nephew of the King.

DEMON PROTECTOR

DORJE CHANG DAY

Each day a supreme pattern in the sky above
the bronze parasol...
Namo Amitabha as the sun sets down in the west
over golf green rice paddy, the earthen landscape
transformed into a lake,
a wooden flute keeps in time with a
red white & blue kite,
swallows feed, the mandala is alive,
flames surround the vajra fence,
inside the lotus circle sits
the sunyata eyes.
I take refuge in the void,
all is void but filled with our
hobbies, but still all is void.
You can see in the eyes that this is true.

The parasol glows above the eyes,
inside is a flame where
Dorje Chang the Vajradhara manifested
and Manjusri made worship and built the stupa.
The sun goes down white tonight like Vajrasattva
who is purified.
I need to be purified.
Myna birds fly over and a mosquito explains
the suffering realms
and the construction of Karma.
I have grown younger and wiser
but i'm growing older.
The feeling of thinking of others before one's
self is the jet motor to the other side
so I fed the mosquito
my blood, whispering
"may all beings be happy."

KEITH DOWMAN, HOLDING TRANSLATIONS

SWAYAMBHU (The all seeing eyes in Nepal)
Blessing Hill through the Seasons

For the view of Swayambhu
we begin the way a four and a half foot Nun
goes round
from sunrise to sundown it takes her
to go around the base of
the holy hill
she moves slowly six feet at a time,
her knees touch the earth, then her hands,
she stretches out in a full prostration,
lays a conch shell where her hands fall
she gets back up
begins her refuge prayer and visualization again
and starts another prostration,
hands cupped they touch her head her throat
her heart center
OM AH HUNG
she goes around like a caterpillar
speaking the names of Buddha, Dharma and Sangha,
she pictures
a pure land her Lama has given her permission
to enter,
in her daily life she struggles to exist
sometimes lost in a fragile body
which any moment causes a lie
or gets diarrhea or disease
her peak time is her refuge prayer
around and round
slowly as a snail
the longer I hang here
the more I see there is nothing more
to do than also fall to the ground
and take refuge.

ༀ

II

The hill is just high enough
to tire you out,
but also you have known from the start of
climbing that you would make it.
You slowly come up to the first Temple which lies
in a saddle to the left of which
is Saraswati & Manjusri Hill, and to the right
Swayambhu, the vajra site,
home of the Dhyani Buddhas
the meaning of Bodhicitta
a place that holds those who hold
the teachings which as you perfect them
enable you to enjoy the fruits of Buddha
CONSCIOUSNESS,
moving in amongst those who know
the grand sciences
the pure arts
and those whose desire is to have you come along,
SWAYAMBHU SWAYAMBHU SWAYAMBHU
UP THE LEFT HAND PATH

Around the corner, stupa next to stupa,
monkeys whose wills are strong,
around the last corner all mind space filled with
the Choten (main stupa) holding full ornaments,
on the left of it a pagoda for the ex-human-eating
mother goddess Harati
turned Dharma protector by Buddha.
There are unknown temples, names forgotten,
I walk up, touch a prayer wheel
and at the point east meet the giant Vajra
at the top of the stairs
then turn and look up at the Choten whose eyes look
at you with a particular awareness
between wrath and peace
which stops the habit
of your mind chatter.
FROZEN LAWLESS BRONZE STUPA
holding some enlightened memory relics,
banners full of mantras wave
and in this center good vibrations
flow from and out to all these suffering realms
OM MANI PADMI HUNG SHRI,
MAY ALL BEINGS BE HAPPY, ROOTED IN HAPPINESS,
OM VAJRASATTVA AH
May they all be Purified
OM AH HUNG
OM AH HUNG
OM AH HUNG
LIKE DIAMONDS.

It draws you on
just like the wheel we're on
but a different one
a type well into the game
of purifying the mind
of all thoughts of a self-existing I
of all thoughts of wanting to get.
It is a river running backwards
but the correct way back
a way of nothingness
full yes you're all the time unendingly there
where? here! there where, there stopping . . .
just another day, just another day
to relive the horror of being in a small mind so little
that it hardly notices or holds its own thought
forms for more than a minute.
Damn it hurts to always wake into a fresh day and feel the heavy
karma of yesterday
so heavy
it's hard to get out of your house.
Meditation is hard
to sit for no reward but a tired back
and a sad view of life with suffering everywhere
with nothing you can do about it
but hope it doesn't get you . . .

Swayambhu where are you oh Swayambhu
sky mind
clouds flowing freely
putting out energy that helps everybody
from man to flea.

A time exists when it doesn't matter what the hell
you do.
You haven't dropped or smoked and the world is
as beautiful as what the eye felt at the dawn
of this creation so...
Death to the Mind Parasites
here is the fortress of the Buddhas
one of the few giant strongholds of Vajrayana

III

I place my prints from one stupa to the next
and think about transcending death.
On the left between Amogasiddhi & Akshobya
is the Tibetan Meditation Palace
inside the colored door is the White Lama and mantras.
The world is not a death trap
his hooded eyes look long at me and I am
not as afraid as I was.
There is no salvation, no idol worship,
only masterpiece sadhanas,
practices that cure one of the dream,
make you aware, out goes the animal.
While crows squawk like alarm clock butlers
sparrows rub their eyes . . .
who is this man a dealer an expert in gold?
I rub my head on the bronze images
and pray munia munia maha munia svaha
I am awkwardly wild
my home is the sky
the proof of my existence is my existence
here is my gold.

The prize is for me to show me
the lost lost jewel rediscovered
become naked as naked
as you are able.
Inside me biting down with fangs
on my lower lip,
hair streaming out, glamorized,
skull tiara.
I look over the edge down on the valley
way far away is Bodnath Stupa,
everything, the houses, the trees, turn into
daisies and ferns
a little Bodnath is in pure land
all places at once,
I am in pure land.
Below   a stone cutter   dit dit dit
cutting on stone   tapping on stone
with a tiny chisel   dit dit dit
he moves his face to me shows a strange
face,   dit dit dit dit dit
Om   dit   Mani   padmi
dit   hung
with his lip hanging loose   cutting in stone
om mani padmi hung
keep up the devotion mr. layman
for when the devotion passes away
the concrete buddhas   will slowly decay
now no museum is Swayambhu swayambhu.

IV

Each season in Nepal is a quick move
the weather fast changing for us living around
the electric dynamo castle
Buddha's guided missile
with a monkey crew
a celestial harmonium spreads
sound from Newari songs shouted…
a ragged Tibetan makes a right hand turn
in his eyes I see harder times for the poor
just as it has always been for without
mindfulness no rock statue
brings warmth & food to the habit
beings who circle.
Even in the overwhelming truth in front of my
entire living breathing thinking jewel
I am blessed to wearily wonder if faith in
the face of golden eyes which say nothing out loud
is enough to keep me going for the rest of my life…
watching the growing weaker ragged monk circle
gets me a lingering question mark
on my christian family upbringing.
All about is the soft humming of this vast
religion.
My name my new name is called from inside the temple,
Sherab Dorje!
I walk back and prostrate myself again
and take refuge in the Buddha Dharma and Sangha.

Namo Amitabha as the sun sets down in
west over green rice paddy,
the earthen landscape transformed
into a lake.
A wood flute keeps time,
swallows feed, the mandala is alive,
flames surround the vajra fence,
inside the mandala maze sits the
lotus circle with burning
sunyata eyes.
I take refuge in the void,
all is emptiness & compassion
filled with our hobbies
but still all is emptiness & compassion.
You and I can see that this is true
by this place's example.

The parasol glows above the eyes.
(No one ever gets away from the eyes once seen.)
Inside is a flame where Dorje Chang the Ati Buddha
manifested and Manjusri made worship and then built this stupa.
The sun goes down white like the skin of
the Vajrasattva who is the purifier.
Bats fly over,
mosquitos explain the suffering realms,
the construction of karma.
I have grown younger and wiser but I'm growing older.
The feeling of thinking of others before
one's self is the jet motor to the
shore so I feed the
hungry ghosts
my flesh
singing and picturing
St Francis
"May all sentient beings
be happy."

V

This earth is tight, its dry mouth and
lips crack showing inner dirt as
dry and brittle as its outside skin
unmoved of course is the stupa
while below we folk
of flesh lay down & push our breath in and out
little do we move in the heat
in a slow way all life is dangerous
temperaments easily lose a sense of compromise
young boys in the cool of the evening
walk back and forth omitting tension
clouds tease us and thunder laughs
a narrow wind carries no water friend.
I lay naked and stare at the gompa's head
outside my window
blowing cool mantras, blowing the conch,tinkling bells
talking to the atmosphere,
no need to go on and tell more of the scene
or how life passes hour by hour,
QUICKSAND!
my galoshes are filled with the stuff,
flutter flutter alter the sputter.

Won't you cuddle my bliss baby?
Because it is only 1/2 grown you can't accept it,
we've been too far away to exchange hellos,
I carry it all to bed in my shallow dreams
and rise with a mantra on my dry lips
to cut the ignorance umbilical cord
when it is not yet quite awake.

jai swayambhu jai swayambhu OM

SWAYAMBHU PHOTO BY A SKY DANCING DAKINI

EASY PREDICTIONS

At the stroke of 4 A. M.
my mind shall become
flayed open
I'll walk over to the Stupa
spin a few prayer wheels
scream at the review
of petty plans with awareness
and still within that awareness
caught in some
hoke-kiss-poke-kiss
warmth, hard woman flesh
enchanted I love this aspect
of my life in hell
and music
the torture of practising
half sour notes and
seeing that the perfect note,
repeated at will,
is 416 light years beyond.

At the stroke of 5 my feet
down the long steps
of Swayambhu
and over to Patan City
in hopes to rub shoulders
with Newars blowing
flutes and beating drums
the natural band on hand
for the bringing out again of the large
bronze Buddhas
of Lokesvara
their hollow innards filled
with the refuge prayers of 100
generations of Newars
Bodhi happy hobbits
aeons of hiding their malas inside
long black velvet sleeves.

What is poetry but action and expressing,
I'm Expressing!
Crimson cartwheels,
ruby mines in the mind of Krishna,
lilliputian politicians
crawling over Gulliver
ten men on his toe
grease oozing between his toes,
subway full of Xmas Packages on their
way to Freeport,
one with a long scar on his
purple jugular vein puts 3 spoons
of sugar in his cup of coffee,
I shan't ever commit suicide
only slowly genocide to my hated sides

Blackbeard
Bluebeard
our hero
Jack the Ripper
at the stroke of this a rise of energy to the
temples, oxygen is sweet and light blue

Hare!
Jai Ho! Boom balay!

P. S. I tell you one strong reason why
them's born in the west howl less.

Shall the weaver of these dreams
    my fabulous senior, overlord dwarf,
        stiletto knife his wisdom sword,
    reveal the X-ray electric radiance now, make it
as easily visible as normal electric flesh...

No human statement can capture as well
    the subtle sound ray flood
        drip this lordly gift:
            the moon, a skull cup half tilted,
                white sperm floats
                    gravity having no hold on it,
        sperm, blood-love
    trees break on the sandscape
        brilliant crow's nest   growing finally into
            a mass of bones amid the sound of invisible
                mouths.
Every atom is screaming down the hill,
               in patch patterns
        the picked forms
            flood in a waterfall,
    there cannot any longer be a need to stick
    to the idea of anything permanent and the
    trick is you can think everything is pemanent
as you roll in your cardboard television box down
    the hill.

From here the thoughts are streaming down
        (into Delhi & Paris)
        people await their coming with a mind
        that's not needed to receive them,

        "here my wounded mothers take
        a round worm in your father's fist
        and i hope it gets you stoned."

                Hare
                Hare to liberation
                    in the sense of a bold screech in the
                        cloud infested night.

DEVOTION

STILL TRYING TO GET ITS ROCKS OFF

or Hungry for Someone Else's Butt

(written by a melting hand on the banks of a rice paddy
in between the vise of 2 Hungry beasts)

The violence crawls,
it's always there,
I can feel it in me,
I can feel it in you reading this,
just the right thing can touch it off.

Forget the justification or the karma rap,
it happens,
and you're either down on the ground
looking up
or on top looking down
in any situation.

And here I sit on the head of a pin as
if the caterpillar from Alice in Wonderland.
If anything drops down i'll be squashed in
the middle of a Who are You rhetoric.
So like I said in the first line,
violence crawls
and it crawls in us all and and
I don't know man, sometimes I get this
hopeless feeling of not being on hand
for the start of Aquarius
but on the front part of Ulysses' arrow.
I do feel this is all illusion but this
clear still solidity of
"can I get this visa or blood on the cover
of Newsweek or starvation in Africa or no money
oh mother and dead father this eternal disciple
crawling like an eel up to crawling on hands and knees
and i'm still afraid of any shadow!"

I throw myself down to be massaged by my brothers
and sisters who as I get to know them better
crawl with me aliened by 100,000 billion
tight jaws, assholes, and tickets for
a train in Patna.

II

the santa claus lady
    who heralded the coming of Karmapa
    for Hopis,
a woman whose only way of hurting someone else
    is by trying to help too much gets
        stoned by men with minds so simple
          that rape is still an adventure
            of caste jumping while drunk

the lamb runs and the family dog smells
    the odor of fear
there is nothing more to do
it is as simple as water running downhill
    the animal goes for the throat
the lamb without a sound is totally
  resigned in desiring to escape
    and having no way to

III

there was a time
when spontaneous joy could be manifested
without thinking of the ramifications
and without any more ado
gone   i'm civilized
    I break out   I'm civilized again
  I break out   I'm civilizated again
etc.
the most sophisticated of civilizers
the one that promises the ultimate break out
captures my flashing child of light poet embodiment.
        you see once you've been
        and now have begun you're trapped into
        finishing and like a dark curse
    a shadow keeps saying,
        "you've been initiated and have
    not carried out the full path's mission.

I'm civilized again…
                         is what's really happening
only happening in my mind?
                    good   grief
what   a strange   experience

SPINNING OF THE WHEEL AT BOUDHANATH

Slowly the wheel turns, the Rinpoche taking his lunch upstairs.
Down here in the main part of the temple is a vein of gold.
A wonderful lustre and soft colors,
monks relax, om manis roll out spontaneous.
Long life and spiritual wealth puja,
Arya Tara.
When a man, a yogi, a reincarnated Lama comes,
he brings with him the entire lineage,
from the very essence.
Hundreds of people's faith and practice climbs degrees
and the wheel spins
the earth is enriched.
At this point which is known as the center one
could say the inner wheel spins,
the eyes of Boudhanath radiate.

A thousand Tibetans are out in the hot sun.
They have come for blessings.
A strong line of Lamas roll into the gomba, and in the rear
Shakya Tenzig,
yogi lama, married with 2 child prodigies
                and speaking good English.
Slowly they sit, he in the front door looking out,
a golden dorje throne,
a golden face wearing a crown,
mantras fall into a microphone,
eye glasses glow in the sun,
the wheel turns, just people a backdrop of trees
            GO SUM GU PEI KYAB SU CHI
            GO SUM GU PEI KYAB SU CHI
            GO SUM GU PEI KYAB SU CHI *

* Refuge Prayer: "Take refuge, respectfully, with our three doors."

DHARMA WHEEL FOOT OF THE BUDDHA

LAMA YESHE PRESIDING

There's a thangka in the meditation tent with a
compassionate man who has
naked people in his hand.
He's so much bigger than
them.
All around beings are doing their thing and when one thinks he
or she's ready the big man says, "yeah
you're ready and now it will be simple.
Close your eyes dear and let
the light of Dharma wash your negativity away, don't
let yourself down, you can develop, you can be free."
Then from some ancient
knowledge he secretly removes a few old skeletons from
your closet, breathes a little Dharma energy into
your nostrils, places his golden hands on your
ears and speaks, "I now pronounce you on your way
to Enlightenment."

TIME TO PRACTISE (Lama Zopa)

Like a little child who has control
    of almost all
I look in the eyes that see so far beyond
    this temporal world.
A happy giggle to insure us all
    that it is possible to get away
    from the ancient hold of ignorance
    which we have suffered from, from beginningless
                time.

Precious Umbrella, heir to Guru Sakyamuni,
        thank you for taking on the hard job
        of teaching us. . .
            slaves of unending suffering.
The spark of pain at the start
    appears so great, but the
realization of what the cost has been
    to gain this perfect human rebirth
erases the pain and makes me strong.
Small man in monk's robes.
    Compassion flowing from your pores.
Ultimate methods for enlightenment fall
    out your mouth.

So easy to build idols
    and not cause for my freedom.

SEPT. 12 SWAYAMBHU IN MIST

Swayambhu invisible in snow piled to the sky
Celestial harmonium and glory to the victorious
                                        Buddha songs drift from up there
                                        somewhere

                7 days ago it was summer
                3 days now rains have poured down
                this morning it's another season

A chill, must put on some wool
the body machine too slow to catch up grinds
                sneezes
        my left lung wheezes

A ragged Tibetan makes the turn at the Bodhi Tree
in his eyes one sees harder times for the poor
it is harder to sleep and starve when damp and threadbare

In the summer, in bright sunshine
when the cuckoo's song is heard
one may go almost naked
but in the winter when the moon brightly shines
thin meat tightens string by cold pointed arrows

Without mindfulness no rock statue
                brings warmth to the habit beings
                                who circle
Faith is good fire but the day is long
        many blows against the small wooden matches

LEPERJI

How do i give a gift to a leper
    with absolute nature?
Do i cure myself of the leprosy
    that is eating away my mind and
    hand it over, will that bring all
    the universal languages together
    and cause a vaccuum to grow around
    the malignant growth that caused in
the first place the leper to be a leper,
the running sore become a young man or a
woman who stole or bore ill will to a
sweet running brook or . . .
    is the leper my guru?
Does his or her eyes instead of mine
    see the absolute?
"If you give I will take freely, and
for the given you may freely relate
to my suffering.
Let it sink in my dear, suffering
                                suffering
                                suffering
the endless silly rounding
                of self-giving."

WALKING THE STREETS OF KATHMANDU

In the illicit back alleys of paradise
    I pass a strange note
    to Elizabeth Taylor
    she wants me to take her to the
    secret Nyingma Lama
    so she can cop a rainbow burger
    I tell you lady
        I'm not into Dharma
        I'm into the satisfying
            of my desires. . .

CRASH
someone throws a tile from the roof
I die laughing
I enter the Seto Machendranath Temple

many men are singing the Bhajan blues,
the bronze filigree, the bells.
Deities dance up into the air
in supreme majestic concentration.
Chenrezig, Shiva, Tara, radiate,
a snow lion with a staff roars the roar
        around,
        anything,
        fuck maybe,
            yeah,
go fuck yourself he says . . .

SAMSARA & NIRVANA (in my life)

yes! cutting the pain so characteristically thin
that each shiver is felt in the most oriental,
the teaching of the Buddha
and the eastern addiction of pure opium.
Pain in the bowels
in a clear dawn of ghost bells
crawling over to the powder line,
sneaking alone like a thief beggar.

meditation conch blowing monks awake

as if violent pain had amounted
enough for me and sleep
which just came is gone again
Enough of this! alone in dawn glow
of western-mind-cursed
the stream-winner-thinker
glorying in a despot's pleasure
of being aware of the incarnation
and this strange holy lineage
I am holder of . . .

down to the fine line of most tightness
and surely the purest
except in both extreme quarters at once
and as the relief rush of pure
Thai juke smooths the screaming cells
Tibetan drums with horns
pull the correct spirit words
to fit the occasion
I put on my gold robes and hold
the right toys, beware judging me
for this is fragile stuff I tell you
in privy

this is prayer.
I mellow from my act of the damned
moth sold to the devil's jar
and wallow in the early rainbows
of Buddha's stronghold,
flirting openly with a conscious cursing
which I can only bestow on myself
if there is just the slighest attachment
to my cruel twisting
game
which I explain to you .

"So pure each end is my friend
that each extreme trend
is welcomed,
I learn to leave my body correctly
and murder slowly each nerve
unwisely,
feeling justified
at the applied opposites
for this movie to thee I write it
so to show no fixed dogma blighted."

Running now bare in my head
dross of gross and airy also,
smashing delightful torture of dogs
they howl at the temple bells crashing
I like their combination
and the silence after
with the beastbird singing
heard as ticks in the void
as herald angels as the light
comes in.

Drum drum horn horn, I know what worlds
            they create for themselves
the better the maker the better the creation
    golden always without a second
            lost to some petty thought
            or speculation.
    Glory Glory, Holy Holy
    in the dawn now I walk amongst all examples of
life and the first greeting is a mother monkey
    cleaning the body of her now newly dead offspring,
she'll hold it and nurse it till a dirty object
        of death stink it shall be,
    all her pain is somewhere covered in her ritual
        as she carries her burden about the hill,
    telling everyone around here one thing,
    "this is suffering in unawareness"
        telling me a question,
    "how glorious you make your burden brother? . . .
        and how alone it is to carry it . . ."

AUTHOR IN ALLEY WITH BASKET 0N HEAD PHOTO BY JOHN CHICK

ATLANTIS VISION

Atlantis Swayambhu vibrantly alive
the three bodies of the Buddha
fully realized.

Look upon it a thousand times
then all of a sudden it moves,
and you know there is more
than the mundane eye.

There's no returning to
your old ways
you've come too far east.

SLOW FLOOD

The clothes washer strolls
in
purity
although impermanent
I know
is even these brazen Himalayas
Job done she smiling goes down towards
the clear river
while her husband makes prostrations
on a boulder behind me
(offering his body to the essence)
This place here is full of the quietest colors
and the brightest eyesights
in a given situation
the delusion stain that held in the plains
equally is seen bright and
exactly
in the light of wisdom blessings from
these mountains

A flock of doves fly by and from
in the back of them
the white snow floods in to
arrest the constant banter
of a fledgling yogi
who sits amazed
at his good fortune

START OF MONSOON, JUST ANOTHER NEPALI AFTERNOON

Gosainkunda peeks
    its head through cloud cover for a brief
Darshan to me
    on Saraswati Hill home,

grey clouds smear the valley in silence,

rain,
            then sun,
    time to slip myself down the Buddhist
    trodden path of monkey heaven
    to Katmandu.

All the way I hum Green Tara's mantra
    until I no longer know with my usual
        consciousness that I'm saying it.
Through the mud and running dung (cutting threw it)
lucid clarity of monsoon atmosphere
I stroll with Green Tara in my heart center,
    her woman's leg caught in readiness
        for a compassion filled action. (jump)

The world is so small, I work in a bookstore
        named Spirit Catcher
and how could I know the bookstore
    would be having a Tara Puja
        this very afternoon.
A Cipati human skull sits on the desk,
 a swami buys a book or 2,
  a sitar player picks his ear,
    2 monks make tormas on a makeshift altar,

young one lights a butterlamp,
the big one starts the hum,
wisdom bells ring,
2 monks 1 american
        in a sudden temple.

Still after 2 years of sadhana
my embarassment arises as I say the mantra
amongst these original practitioners of Tantra.
I am the total beginner, they are the direct
disciples of the lineage.

Tara isn't Tibetan,
Tara is the Compassion of a Buddha, the teardrop of Bodhicitta,
the soft caress of somewhere's waterfall of bliss.
OM TARE TU TARE TURE SOHA

OM

SUN AND MOON

BHAIREB PHOTO BY IRA COHEN

CRIPPLED BLOOD

Coming away from the feet of Urgyen Tulku
we stroll consciously up the steps of
Boudhanath Stupa.
There on the top step surrounded by French
tourists a crippled boy and friends
torture a sparrow,
it's fun to watch the grimy beggar kids
until one smashes the sparrow like
a piece of wet cloth
and the blood comes out of its
insides
comes out of its mouth
and it's dead.

I enjoy the grim lesson
under the giant sunyata
eyes of Buddha.

MY NEW HOUSE

Out the window the world is roaring
          all the many seas wave in succession
                              crashing
                              crashing
          I am still blessed!
all this past dragon year
my life like a novel
full of life pain concrete
               robot brothers and sisters
          drugs
          and sleeping awareness

          I am in love
           She loves me back
            I am blessed
          as the ice age slowly crawls into
               Europe and America
          I am in paradise i call my home that

all the prophecies from
all the true prophets are true

Kali Yuga obit we travel on to destruction
     and rejuvenation,
ice age, drought, violent death
               in tantra
               adventure.

POKHARA VISION I

In this alone concrete
and bed and sheets
I dream the soaked with sweat
true dreams
I dream of dark tangled shapes
black forms of many kinds
they torture me they are mine
I make them
then to my surprize I find
other people like to have them
and I see them
but I am the maker creator I am
the blackest of them
then these two beloved Lamas come
and I speak to them like I have not
been able to
I see my 2 troubles:
people like others to express
their torture.
and all I really wanted to do was
to be able to communicate with
the Lamas.

Bodhidharma sat till his bottom
went rotten: what a lovely
smell his enlightenment.

In the divine temple of vulva
The tongue of the skillful lover
Mixing white and red seed,
Drinks the nectar of swollen lotus,
Circumambulating the emptiness.

EARTH & HEAVEN

When you say you love me
    do you know its not forever,
when your thigh is showing…

Ahh everything takes so long,
    desire to know all at once,
not pouring the empty into the void.
If the lock's not on my door
    you can sure come in, anytime,
I'll change my study over to you
    mind and body
    and you can enter mine,
nothing is so important
as the sweet transmission
nothing so full of interest as the discourse
        of love in the open
          mind to mind
          skin to skin

2.

please think that the feelings you feel
as we congeal
is heaven's nectar
washing both our minds and bodies clean

Let's dedicate the feelings to all beings
and the raw sex can be holy.
The silk scarf of your breast,
the soft hair on the lobe,
the feathers of the flying mouse
could fly into my mouth,
no mind could denounce it.

You open and i
enter without using a finger
and we sigh
into the wonderful miracle
of completeness.

also

RECEPTIVE & CREATIVE
SPONTANEOUS INTERACTION

DARSHAN from every ATOM

STILLNESS IN ACTIVITY
IT IS NEVER ONLY PENETRATION
IT IS NEVER ONLY ENCIRCLEMENT.

KEITH REDMAN

NOVEMBER 7TH SCORPION

I have a lot
    of fear of death
    fear of burning up the life
    in pursuit of the real
From a birth just before winter
    I find myself still happening
    but the life breath grasped
    has to shorten with each gasp
And I fear before
    the simple dynamo of energy
    is explored to its source
    I will have blundered too many times
    in the web of the status quo
Today I am in my environment
    moist mushroom rotting trees
    a waterfall yellow leaves
    an aura of pink
    to breathe in.

November late Oct. highly emotional
    just before everything dies
at my age
    I feel like November
    my friends feel like November
we like the color
but we want to die to it all
    and become eternal.

GENTLEMAN WITH WALKING STICK

BUYING A WALKING STICK IN PURI

Sir, I would like to buy a pilgrim's stick,
and being that I am not a tourist, I
cannot pay a tourist's price.
So, sir, this is the truth of my situation:
If you can lower your price to a pilgrim's
price, I may buy a stick that I will keep
unto death or until the parting of the stick
and my life.
I must also tell you that I would like the stick to be
one of my choice. Not one a tourist would place
above the fireplace or with the umbrellas.
I need a sturdy stick, one that will help me
pull myself up a hill and through a creek.
One that will hold me up on the top
or on the other side.
So sir, you see my position, and the position
required,
with perhaps a little give and take, we can
make a trade?
Some stick grown, picked and made.
Some money made and paid.
And in some far off time a tale to tell as the stick is
passed down.

ASHES & FLASHES

In a Shiva moon dream,
    to my left shoulder 2 bodies smolder
to my right they carry a person
    about to die toward the temple

blue smoke blows toward drumbeat
        inside Pashupati Nath, Shiva's
        House

        on the parapet I sit, the
        fantasy fort, below the slow running
        holy river,
        birds sing among thousands of statues,
        lotus flower round bull image under
        flying Garudas over rock lingams

the person who died is now a pile of
            wood and bones neatly swept,
the family men are all newly shaven headed
            and sit watching the river
              the smoke
            the amazing ashes which yesterday
            lived with them
I rise clay chillom to forget to be me
    to see with a clear eagle eye the mean truth . . .
        the shadow I carry talks to me,
            I awake before language starts to speak
                in my dreamstate.

Awake I am definitely left alone with . . .
with, with, with the subtle fear which causes
me to protect merely the space around my body
the very air
that surely as the next breath is a black hole
leaving hardly a way to experiment
the sun is hot and I am addicted to my flesh an
addict to living my personal life without strange
changes I don't ask for
the smoke inside my head beating with blood
against my temples in hot sun of many bird voices
and the ringing of words in different languages
in this life a bridge to cross . . .
the burning person is gone
she is only a puddle of grey ashes which turn black
when finally delivered to the river
Shiva's drum is my heartbeat
his bull vehicle is the roaring life in me
poetry coming out
river and muse running down the walls of
the parapet my body and her ashes are white
smoke coming out of the water
flowing down to the Ganga the Bay of Bengal
The Pacific
and America.

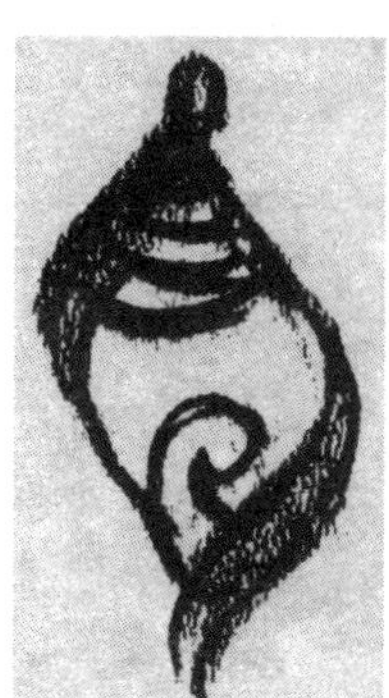

SON of the SUN OF DHARMA

I had this dream
    Chökyi Nyima Rinpoché and me
                in a museum
    Suddenly we start breaking statues
then we have to run for it
    Chökyi Nyima in his robes
    he turns and says "that was breaking limits"
a white motorcycle appears and Chokyi jumps
on and starts it,
tells me "get on, you know let's go"
we're going as fast as light
        down a thin road,
he turns and tells me
    "fear doesn't exist."

CHOKYI NYIMA RINPOCHE

BODHISATTVA

A LONG LIFE PRAYER FOR CHOKYI NYIMA RINPOCHE AND KHENPO TSEWANG GYATSO RINPOCHE

LINDA ?, ROBERT BEER, TANCHA WHITFIELD, ROBERTO VALENZA ON MEDICINE BUDDHA PILGRIMAGE

IDLE REFLECTIONS OF KOPAN

Ah, sitting relaxed in my little room
        dabbing paint
        now & then on a rice print of
                Palden Lama
and it hits me how cool the Bodhisattva is,
too strong it would be, too cold and cruel
to come out and say
"when you get old you begin to smell like
rotted cloth,
and everyone knows your time will come soon."
No! what the true buddy tells is the
        story of the long-life gods
        and their downfall,
he lays it out there
with a serious face
and a jackal's laugh inside his sleeve.

WINGS & WOUNDS

The crows sometime come
    and speak to the bats,

hanging upside down and stretching
        black silk wing of
        chicken bone arm
            the bat crawls below . . .
            then pulls itself up
    and stands on top of
    eucalyptus menthol branch

there you are hanging on your tree
    your shaven arms surprize me,
        little queen the whole
    thing will fall and you'll still
        be hanging upside down
    I will always love you
                that's the rule

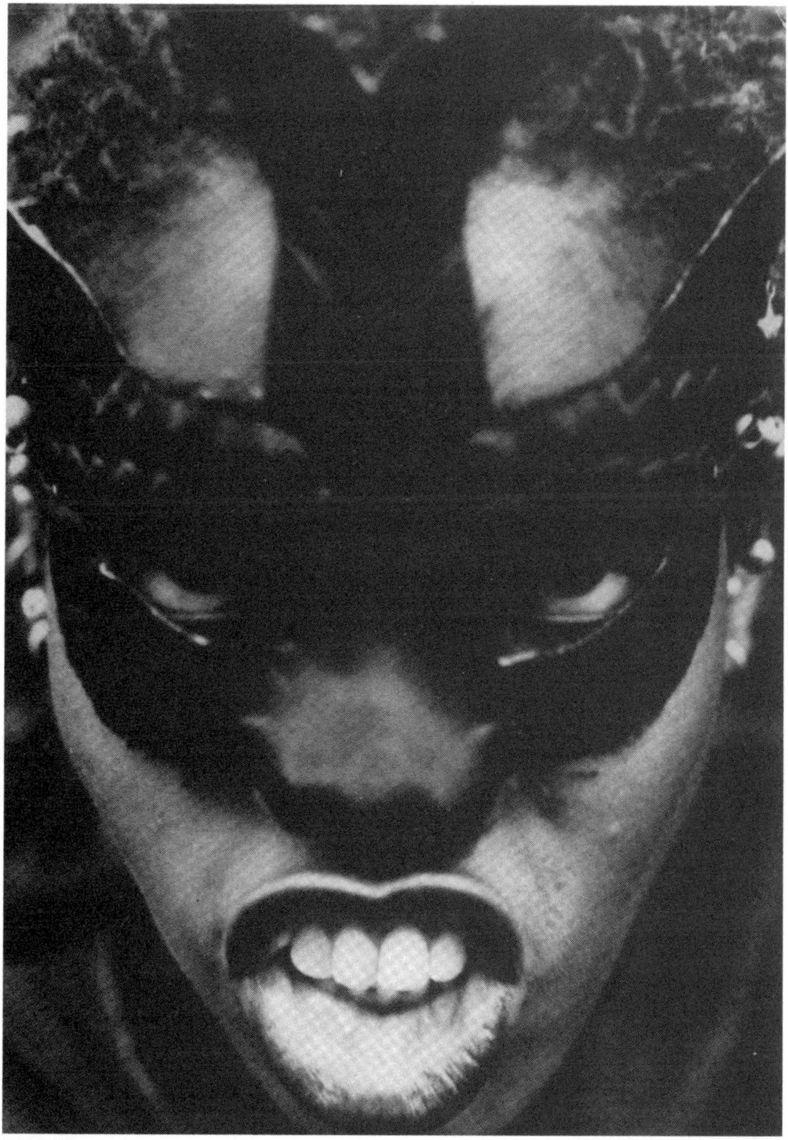

DIEDER PHOTO BY IRA COHEN

VERSE COLLECTED FROM 3 WEEKS AT THE REX HOTEL IN BOMBAY

bent noises, basic advertising, the importance
    of handouts plus the power of continuity...
an untouchable pile of drifting dirty people
    flow like river debris under the neighborhood
tourist hotel window,
puppy youth learn who's big,
the fat lady with her flea filled monkey baby,
see her swing it in the air by its collared neck
and laugh as its eyes bug out and he runs
under her rotting orange dress,
she listens to the mattress fixer fellow
    & hears the twinge of his machine,
    she watches a girl scout begging rupees from
        a tourist youth,
        all day it never stops this slow fight
            with starvation,
                in this noise world under the window
                    of the outlaw Rex Hotel.

a dreaming sparrow tries again to find a voice
that sounds like bird song
he could be Caruso but he keeps on
only remembering that he's just a simple sparrow

a red double decker bus carries England within itself,
this morning is a damp burden for an overpacked tourist
not finding a taxi,

and the chinese junkie keeps losing his coins
by never remembering he's got holes in his pockets,
ghosts are in fashion, they haunt New India,

II

this morning 3 cops hold the arms of a man
with a towel around his middle, for a strange
moment the street has silence then the explosion
of life carries on.
crows are the singers here,
singers of fear & greed & jealousy,
but mostly laughter at the cost of some other.

morning rat shit...
out in the road a french flip-out walks the white line
playing insane dodge-em car games with death,
the trouble mornings, boring moooorning,
heavy lung morning full of farewell...

2 motor scooters at the curb look to be 2 butlers
waiting for "me lady"
while antique autos live forever under coconut palms

III

There is this morning down below the window
one of the families of acrobats, one by one they do
the same tricks with their kids, throwing them around,
passing them through flaming hoops,
jumping through, tying them to poles,
hoping someone will throw down at least some
painful charity so they can eat,
I throw some down, at least they are working,
they are better than those who sing the lying song,
"No momma, no poppy, no food, money,"
they keep old dirt on
not washing ever they stay a beggar,

it's a nitty gritty mandala down there,
people screaming, people falling on their faces,
some supporting, others parasites

IV

crow squeak, early morning talk…
dog bark, early morning noise,
one trillion sparrow tongues ricochet
  off the walls of buildings,
truck engines roar making it out onto the highway,
  the street sleepers wake & mourn
      into another dawn,
    it's hard to be stomached from an
      empty yesterday that is tomorrow
                    this morning,
I go to refuge,
    good morning world! good luck to you!
I throw water into the face and wash yesterday's
    race down the sink,
  I kiss the garden that is my woman
and give thanks to the fact the she breathes
    next to me,
    unafraid of what the morning news
          will scream
    and I don't know
      the whole day
      like the day before

V

the street is owned by the sound of sweeping
and a tapping like in the carving of stone rock,
living is the
car motors & the beeping of horns,
the slick hawk glides over the scene with a
vicious eye, he's an awe inspiring
figure which no other animal but
the gang of crows will mess with.
oh waking into a morning of dreams,
a solid wall of tweetering metal music of birds,
a strange roar as if this concrete place were
yawning good morning.
An invisible giant with his foot on my chest
is pressing his foot on me
causing my breath to come hard,
uneasy...
A warlock downstairs i know he's down
there with a beverage
that will remove
this heavy foot plus
allow me to move in this world of engines
that's speeding all day without stopping.
I should go down to him
but there's a spell on the door
in a language
I know not how to read...
maybe if I close my eyes
CHANGE will come & stay this owner of the foot,
lead me into a different day dream,
softly I drop my guard...

V I

I got today the bloodshot stare
creeping between events & I'm looking down
at the street for the next to last time,
yes I'm moving on.
this morning the hotel guards are slapping around
the beggar babies,
& and the crows have a wicked voice,
there is definitely no world for me today
until coffee comes

to look out the window at all the weirdos
is one thing
but to walk amongst them is more a personal touching thing,
their hands pointing at me & then them
singing "no money, no mommie no poppie
give food and coin"
also a young Charles Boyer says "give me
2 rupees for my morphine,
better for me you understand"

this morning I know cigarettes are killing me
cigarettes, dampness & silver needles...
leaving this beautiful home for another tomorrow,
going far far away from these beggar streets
of Bombay.

COW RECEIVING BLESSING IN STREET

BODHISATTVA VOW TAKEN

Who are the teachers glorious,
        the sky & mind fliers . . .

    growing up out of childish pursuits,
        if it is a Buddha's mind
        I desire to become
    then if and when i call for help
        I should be sure to know
        the ways to call . . .
    and know the nature
        of their power:

the soft soft heart,
    that speech that's sweet
    or hard
        to fit the moments of many forms . . .
  to these natures I bow down
    and ask sincere for
        your help and blessing
so that I may be one less in the suffering
                                realms
        and one more of those who vow
   to keep the mind in different forms
      till there is no more
         suffering to be found.

JOY

it doesn't matter what you do, or
 where you go, it matters how you
 do it.
Karma is mental, and how is the
 vibration, you cannot learn to
 help others if you always are
 cherishing yourself.
Look inside for the feeling, not just
 outside at what you are seeing.
It's such a joy to wake up.
 Good morning.
Please dedicate feelings and merits
 to the Enlightenment of all beings.

SPIRIT CATCHER INK PEN DRAWING BY ROBERT BEER

Oh yes, Rose Hips

Was it in Sparta
or volcanic Jakarta
perhaps the roof of the
Grace Hotel Kathmandu,
that I first saw those peaches
ripe from the tree of life,
Holy Christ,
Bless me Buddha,
they were nice…
then the feet oh so neat
walking with black nail polish,
on pins of ivory,
my my my it was exciting.
Yes, yes, yes, it was Rose Hips
they were, she was,
call me Rose Hips,
odd though it is I can't remember
the spot on earth I first saw her.

It seems a tall man with the
coat hanger shoulders, glasses,
a drummer of sorts, into being a dervish
was about.
Well then again
there was at that time a dark bard
with his lady in black,
her skulls and silver,
I hung on her every motion
she wasn't Rose Hips
that's for certain,
Dracula's daughter perhaps but Rose Hips no!
not that sweet sturdy wench Rose Hips
as if the word itself were sugar watered
and big and broad as all out of doors.
Yes it's the beginning to come,
it was the Yak & Yeti Restaurant,
Boris was holding court with his Romeo son Ken
doing the lights,
their Beef Stroganoff was a Bonanza
during the the winter months

and Rosey loved the vegetables
brought up by Border Tribe folk
about 4 foot tall
romantic they were like being in prehistoric times
with a chandelier on angel dust,
it was quite a sight
and just a long jump to the
Hot Springs by the Chinese Border.
But something tells me it wasn't there
that I first saw her.
What about Goa? She dancing
naked on the beach to the Birmingham boys
on Strats plus
Steve, Terry and myself on wind instruments.
I can almost picture it, that strawberry hair of hers
everywhere and the sea rocking & rollin
like the giant blob.
Eek! It was in Peshawar!
It was the time the police told us opium was bad
and the entire Market Place laughed at them
as we blew brown smoke towards Mecca.
Where are you Rose Hips?
That smiling face and those cheeks?
What sea are you near as I lap the fallow memory
cells that hold you somewhere
where I might find you once again
and hold you to my chest and kiss your
sunburned face?
Do a tea ceremony,
set up the flowers quite correctly,
heat the water over hot coals
and place your hips into the fresh water,
drink you down like the nectar you are,
sip you with my pinkie out,
envision you in every party spot
from America to Bali and back,
with the day dreaming of an addict.

UNMASKING

This club I've joined got their price of admission.

Nay, nay, speak not to me of how the spiritual kingdom is.

Gliding through white diamonds of explanation,
a moist gentle kiss
...the natural voice speaks syllables...
visitors come and go speaking of rebellion...

Amazing the energy of loving free space.
I look at you from the subject to object and you're on a
picture screen that holds my interest in a gay sort of way
like building sand castles for art's sake or a fiery romance
to stir the heart of life...

my coat out I spin
the screen around me spins
I'm inside a prayer wheel
I say mantras   I hummmm
I break out in song singing...
arms up in the air
air particles are stars   hoo-ray   hoo-ray
I am part of this peak time
the part shooting through nothing but this...
stretching to realms and realms of adventure in full.
My coat out I spin
the screen around me spins
as in a prayer wheel   I say mantra
I hum   Om Ah Hung
I break out screaming   wailing   singing

LIVING IN THE VISUALIZATION

I am a vocal being, a multi-creative being, a singer in many types of musical collaborations, writing the songs, reading the poems. Wherever I have lived I either start or help out with poetry readings and open mic opportunities. Taking part in the ancient oral and written tradition of poetry, I am also a painter, chapbook maker, photographer.

All of these forms have a foundation of Tibetan Buddhist practice with some alchemy thrown in. Sex is certainly an important surrendering practice, much like all the rest of the many art forms. The poems here are an important part of the sharing I desire to place within the short life span we all have. The poems and songs in *Under The Precious Umbrella* are my living baby steps. My awe still comes alive as I read them, my knowledge of how huge my good fortune was and is to have met teachers, the Dharma, and a helpful Sangha.

The poems are naive, sometimes innocent, enthusiastic and curious, virtues I need still. It is a long road through samsara until finally meeting a way out of ignorance. My practice is not as strong as it should be, but my faith and devotion in the 3 vehicles is large, more powerful than I acknowledge. So if you are reading these, see them as seed, freshly thrown on the soil of Vajrayana. It could be that these poems are your first sight with a down to earth vision, from a streetwise character like myself. There can be no better way to live than to share goodness, be a Goodhist.

Please feel free to communicate with me on these poems or other artistic subjects.

Email robertovalenza@hotmail,com
www.gulfcoastyoga.com

2001 Year of the Snake

Roberto Valenza

PHOTO OF ROBERTO VALENZA BY DONNA LEE

many of these poems appeared in *poems for the glancing eye*; *mandala of poems, maha kala in the center*; or *precious umbrella*, chapbooks published by nine muses books under the general title of *The American Tibetan Poems and Songs of Sherab Dorje*.

typeset in HELVETICA to correspond with the earlier chapbooks, this book, like the chapbooks, was designed by Roberto Valenza and margareta waterman; the covers designed by Donna Lee and Roberto Valenza. back cover design taken from an old tibetan coin. the illustrations, drawings and photos, were prepared for print by Donna Lee.

manufactured in oregon: text printed by EugenePrint in eugene; cover and flysheets printed by Douglas Fir Printing in roseburg; PUR binding by Lincoln & Allen in portland.